1984

THEY CAUGHT THESE KILLERS

THEY CAUGHT THESE KILLERS

By

BRUCE SANDERS

ROY PUBLISHERS, INC.
NEW YORK 10021

Library of Congress Number 69-14164

PRINTED IN GREAT BRITAIN

For
the other Bruce
who will know why
and may be amused

CONTENTS

FOREWORD

The appeal of the fictional detective story in the category of sensational reading entertainment is surpassed, perhaps, only by the extra stimulation afforded by the best true-crime stories.

All things else being equal, fact will usually prove more arresting and more exciting than fiction for one overriding reason.

It actually happened.

And just as history is admitted to be capable of repeating itself, so can crime—and it often does. So that what has occurred may occur again, and the repeat performance may conceivably engulf the reader and change his or her life in a terribly dramatic manner.

For human beings are notoriously imitative, and what one has another acquires, what one acquires another wants. Also, what one does another frequently wishes to do.

If humans were not imitative to a sometimes frightening degree fashion creators and designers would starve, and from all accounts they are currently very far from becoming possible future subjects for Oxfam appeals. If they were, perhaps one might be disposed to give more generously.

However, the cases included in this book are each unique in its way as a combined murder and consequent manhunt. The crimes narrated and the detective triumph related to the finding of the killers are, in their own right, originals. They do not offer, in any sense, imitations of other true-crime cases. For this value alone they have achieved international fame of sorts and certainly profound recognition among criminologists. Such value apart, they are all strong human dramas, with a full range of emotions extending from revulsion to pathos, from admiration to horror.

They are, in short, cross-sections of our civilization, and to a greater or lesser degree we are all caught up in their implications because they happened. They portray a way of life and death that could have been ours in changed circumstances. Therein lies the special appeal, one that is almost hypnotic at times.

Yet in sequence the crimes outlined here provide a diverse catalogue of human violence that is in no sense repetitious, for the takers of life demonstrated ingenuity, subtlety, and perseverence, admirable human qualities debased by unworthy use.

Fortunately those same qualities are to be found in more than equal measure in the men commissioned by society to find and bring to retribution the outlaws who both denied and defied the creed that human life is sacred to all men.

Thus, necessarily, these cases are shown in strong contrasts of light and shade, the basic lighting scheme for all powerful human drama. That I knew a few of the actors on this crime stage personally gives me a feeling occasionally of peering round a colourful backdrop behind that stage or overhearing a voice offstage in the wings.

This I have allowed to intrude into these pages, hoping in this way to pass on to the reader some deeper appreciation of a man who was real enough and big enough in his time to make his own piece of police history.

1

THE CASE OF THE STOCKING PRINT

John Sands was a man with a big frame, a big jutting jaw, and a big grin. Some years after he had retired as one of Scotland Yard's detective superintendents, and when he was organising security for the Epsom Grand Stand Association, I asked him which of his cases he remembered as the most outstanding manhunt.

There was no hesitation in his reply.

"The Wimbledon lovers' lane case," he said. "That one gave me some bad moments. I needed some luck—just a little. But it took a long time arriving."

The lovers' lane he referred to was a narrow thoroughfare not far from the All-England Lawn Tennis Courts. At each end the black letters on the white name-plate spelled out the words Somerset Road. It was a street noted as a local rendezvous for courting couples.

On Thursday, July 14th, 1938, it was a scene of violent death. The man who made the grim discovery was a fireman attached to the Kingston Fire Brigade. His name was John William Love —a fact not without some irony in the circumstances. It was in the early hours of the morning that he was driving along Somerset Road on his way home. His headlights threw a broad beam of light over the grass verge running the length of the narrow road. Suddenly the light swept across a dark object that the fireman thought, at first glance, was part of a fallen tree. But as his car came closer he saw the dark object had arms and legs.

John Love stopped his car and walked towards the grass verge. He found himself staring down at the body of a young woman dressed in black. There was blood on her face, and she had obviously been brutally beaten about the head. The fireman stopped long enough to make sure she was dead, and then he hurried back to his car and drove off to inform the police of what lay in their local lovers' lane.

As it happened, he did not have far to drive, for after travelling some three hundred yards he saw a police car. It was not many minutes later that the local divisional detective inspector, John Henry, was awakened in his home by the ringing of his telephone.

The familiar voice of a station sergeant informed him, "A woman's body has been found in Somerset Road, Wimbledon. It's murder."

Another detective roused from sleep that early morning in mid-July was my friend the late Fred Cherrill, who later retired from Scotland Yard as the chief superintendent in charge of the Fingerprint Bureau. In the summer of 1938 Fred Cherrill was a chief inspector. Some light was flushing the sky when Cherrill and Henry and a group of other police officers began a grisly examination.

The victim of a savage attack wore a black dress, black shoes, and black gloves. She was found lying on her back, her face masked with blood, which had pooled on the grass under her head. There were ragged cuts in the flesh of her face, and it was plain that she had been attacked by someone who had turned on her suddenly, taking her off guard. A number of deep and ugly wounds had been inflicted on her skull.

The most interesting feature of the wounds, to the experienced eyes of the group of police officers studying the battered head in the light of several torches, was the apparent pairing of the lacerations. Each pair was the same distance apart. This suggested a possible weapon to Fred Cherrill.

"A car's starting handle could have made them," he told the others bending over the dead woman.

Later that grim moment of insight was remembered by Cherrill because just as he bent down closer he was startled by the sudden liquid sound of a blackbird greeting the dawn. The country-bred expert on fingerprints later recalled his feelings very vividly.

"I knelt down beside the body to make a closer examination," he recorded, "and as I did so the liquid notes of a blackbird, perched on the low-hanging branch of a tree overhead through which the light of dawn was just beginning to filter, broke the eerie silence of the morn. It was a plaintive, melancholy song, incongruous yet somehow in keeping with that tragic moment. One might almost have thought that this bird was singing a requiem for the dead girl beside whom I was kneeling."

It was on the inside of the stocking on the dead woman's right leg, not far above the ankle, that a clue was found by the searching police. This was some marks made by a motor vehicle's tyre. The marks showed very clearly the tread of the tyre.

They were, in fact, a stocking print.

As Cherrill himself saw it, judging from the angle at which the body was found lying, the vehicle had been driven diagonally across the road so that a wheel had passed over the victim at right angles. This surely was a further indication of brutal callousness on the part of the killer.

"I'd like to have that stocking later," Cherrill said to his colleagues. "I think it could prove useful."

That made him, within the space of a few minutes, right on two separate counts. The murder weapon did prove to be a car's starting handle, as he explained to Dr. Gardner, the pathologist, and the stocking print helped more than any other single clue to produce the eventual solution to that lovers' lane murder.

However, if the killer had left a stocking print behind, he had been careful to take with him the dead woman's handbag, containing immediate means of identification. Moreover, the police searchers found no sign of a hat that had been dropped by the victim as she fell under a rain of blows.

Another feature of the discovery of the corpse in Somerset Road was the absence of any signs of a struggle or scuffle. The soft earth of the grass verge was not dug up with footprints. Indeed, the victim's legs had been off the grass and on the road when the wheel rolled over the right calf, leaving the stocking print. There were no spattered bloodstains, only the muddy pool of drying blood under the battered head.

It looked very much as though the victim had been killed elsewhere and her body conveyed to this lonely lane and dumped in a hurry, which would have been consistent with the wheel bumping over the right leg that was left on the road. The killer had been in a hurry to be away.

Of course, there was an alternative, and not a pleasant one. The killer could have driven over her leg deliberately to give the false impression that she had been hit by a passing car.

But no passing car had caused those injuries to her head.

The body of the murdered unknown was removed by ambulance to the local mortuary, where it was examined by Dr. Eric Gardner, who made the post-mortem. He had his own quota of information to add to what the police had discovered in Somerset Road. The victim had not only been bludgeoned about the head. She had received a number of stab wounds. Her death was due to her multiple injuries.

The stocking with the print of a tyre's tread was carefully removed from the crushed leg and packed for dispatch to Scotland Yard, where it was unwrapped and examined afresh by Fred Cherrill through a powerful lens. He decided the pattern of the tread was clear enough to be photographed.

Meantime the Wimbledon police were trying to discover the victim's identity. The injuries to her head and face had made identification difficult, for any policeman who might have known her features in life would be puzzled to recognise them in the slashed face of the victim.

Cherrill had taken her fingerprints, but already he had checked that they were not on file in his department. By mid-morning Wimbledon Common was being combed by squads of searching police who sought any clue pointing to where the victim could have been murdered. The morning passed with no useful report being sent in.

A conference was held at Scotland Yard. The Chief Constable of the Criminal Investigation Department, John Horwell, attended with the area superintendent and the divisional detective inspector. When it broke up a description of the dead woman was prepared and handed out to the Press. An official request was made for anyone who recognised the description to come forward and help the police.

With the description went a mock-up photograph of the dead woman, a piece of photography that, in its own way, was a brilliant professional job, for the Yard men had to reconstitute, as it were, the murdered woman's battered face. Another generation had to pass before identikits were being regularly used.

As the result of the Press publicity and the radio announcements made by the B.B.C. people began coming forward who believed they could identify the dead woman. While most of them failed to name her, a name was eventually supplied. It was Rose Muriel Atkins.

The dead woman, as a few of the police on the case had already surmised, had been a prostitute. Her home was a small flat in Putney Bridge Road, about a mile and a half from where her body was found. She had been known to her acquaintances and customers as Irish Rose, and to some as simply Pat, for she had spoken with a noticeably Irish accent.

The detectives on the case began filling in the lost hours of Irish Rose's last day. She had been seen to leave her flat dressed in a distinctive style of black tailored suit with a black fur that had a tail with a sharply contrasting white tip. To complete her stylish ensemble she wore a white hat of some open-work material and lace gloves through which the flesh of her hands could be seen.

Irish Rose had been a smart dresser on the day she died in such a terribly bedraggled fashion.

She called in at a club in Clapham High Street in the afternoon and did not leave until five o'clock, when she was thought to have returned home, for she was known to be in her flat in the first part of the evening.

By ten o'clock there was still some light in the July sky. That was the time she was seen to alight from a bus along Parkside, Wimbledon. She would have caught the bus only a few yards from her front door. It was soon after she had left the bus in Wimbledon that she ran into a man she knew slightly. He told the police she had told him she was down on her luck and wanted to make some money in a hurry.

She had invited him to return to her flat.

He had refused, but had given her some change he found in his pocket because he felt sorry for her and she had admitted her purse was empty.

When she walked on after stopping this man Irish Rose had four shillings in her handbag.

However, the inquiring detectives had to cover a good deal more ground, and make inquiries of many more people, before they came upon the female witness who admitted she had seen Rose Atkins alive an hour and a half after the meeting at ten o'clock. That put the time at eleven-thirty.

According to this new witness Rose Atkins was seen by her standing at a street corner, where Inner Park Road ran into Parkside. She had known Irish Rose for some time, and was on the point of crossing the road to have a chat with her when a small green tradesman's van drew up and braked opposite Rose Atkins. The woman on the street corner sauntered up to the van driver and was seen talking to him. A couple of minutes later she climbed into the seat beside him and the van drove off.

The direction it took led towards Somerset Road, the local lovers' lane.

The woman who had observed this had walked on down Parkside, unaware that she had seen Irish Rose alive for the last time or that she was, in fact, the last person to see the unfortunate woman alive save her murderer.

It was this piece of eye-witness evidence that switched the Yard inquiry to London's multitude of small green vans. Several hundred were looked over for bloodstains and the stories of their owners and drivers checked. Additional evidence suggested that Irish Rose's story of being flat broke might have been somewhat wide of the truth, for a number of women who knew her told the police that she had a secret pocket built into the lining of her white-tipped fur, and she was known to carry, at various times, a fair sum in that unsuspected pocket. As much as forty pounds was mentioned.

By this time the police had also discovered Rose Atkins' age. She was thirty. She was also married and had had two children.

But she died penniless, for there was no wad of folding money in the secret pocket of her fur when the police found it, and as her handbag had vanished it was not difficult to suspect the motive for the crime—robbery.

The checking of light green vans extended beyond the Metropolitan Police area to the remainder of England and Wales when the London van investigation drew blank. That was when Fred Cherrill performed in his small office at Scotland Yard like a magician.

"With the aid of my hand lens," he related later, "I discerned on the stocking in my possession the pattern of the tread of a motor-car tyre. I had a photograph taken of this tread, and armed with this visited a number of firms dealing in motor tyres."

It was Fred Cherrill, pounding his own specialist's beat, who came up with an important piece of information that suddenly narrowed the search for the green van.

"I found that tyres of that particular size," he said, "were fitted only to cars of the Austin Seven or Morris Eight type."

On the morning of Saturday, July 16th, a Mr. Boseley walked into the police station in Tottenham Court Road. He voiced a complaint. A driver employed by him to deliver parcels of repaired shoes and boots had decamped with the sum of thirty-two pounds that he had collected on the 14th. The man had been warned that failure to pay in the sum collected would mean the police being informed. Mr. Boseley had had similar trouble previously with the driver, whose name was George Brain. The sergeant in the police station duly wrote down the particulars supplied by Mr. Boseley, including Brain's address. The missing driver had apparently lived with his parents in Richmond.

Then the station sergeant did a quick double-take. For Mr. Boseley was saying, "The van he took is a Morris Eight. The colour's green."

What Mr. Boseley did not have to explain was that Richmond lies to the west of Putney and not far from Wimbledon. However, he did explain that Brain's reason for having the use of the green van was to ferry another employee from the firm's boot- and shoe-repairing premises in Pancras Street to his home in Twickenham. After dropping this man, Frost, Brain would continue in the van to Richmond. The next morning he would pick up Frost and drive on to Pancras Street.

When Mr. Boseley's news was passed on to the Scotland Yard men on the case they called on Frost, who told them he had been picked up by George Brain, in the usual way, on the morning of the 14th.

That was within a few hours of Rose Atkins being killed.

As Frost climbed into the seat beside Brain he smelled dampness and looked around. The inside of the van had been washed out since he had left it the previous evening.

Later that same day Brain had collected the missing thirty-two pounds. He should have handed it in on the Friday morning. When he failed to do so he was given the warning about having it paid in by Saturday morning if he didn't want the police to be told.

The shoe-repair business opened on the Saturday morning, and at the usual time Brain had picked up Frost, but while driving over Twickenham Bridge he had suddenly stopped and got out.

"What's up?" Frost asked.

"I'm going away somewhere," Brain told him, and without another word had turned and hurried away.

Frost had stared after him in amazement. After Brain had disappeared from view the other man climbed over into the driving seat and continued the drive to Pancras Street.

It was the D.D.I. at the Tottenham Court Road police station, Peter Beveridge, who precisely two years later was to arrest Mrs. Florence Iris Ouida Ransom for the "white gloves" multiple shooting in a Kentish orchard, who hurried to the garage where Frost had left the green van. Although the interior had been washed out, as Frost had explained, the work had been done hurriedly, and Beveridge found dried bloodstains on the floor. He phoned the news to Jack Henry, who called at Brain's home, to learn that his parents had not seen their son George since he had left with the van as usual that Saturday morning.

Henry also learned that, on the night of Irish Rose's murder, Brain had not returned home until well after midnight.

George Brain was suddenly wanted by the police, and not only to return Mr. Boseley's missing thirty-two pounds. For in a small room, not much larger than a cubby-hole, behind the garage containing the green van with bloodstains on the floor was found a handbag.

It was Irish Rose's.

According to Fred Cherrill, the manhunt now mounted was one of the most sensational he could remember. As he put it, "A hue and cry was raised for George Brain which echoed from Land's End to John o' Groat's."

For nine days any unfortunate man who resembled George Brain was liable to be stopped and asked to make a statement at the local police station. He was also asked for his fingerprints. For on Irish Rose's handbag Cherrill had found a "foreign" fingerprint. It was one that looked masculine to Cherrill's knowing and experienced eye, but it could not be checked because George Brain, the wanted man, had no criminal past and his fingerprints were not on file.

All the fingerprints taken of men answering to George Brain's description failed to supply one that matched the "foreign" print reposing on Cherill's desk in a photographic enlargement.

The whole of the Richmond and Wimbledon areas, with their vast open spaces, were searched closely by hunting policemen looking for a body. For as day succeeded day with no real news of the genuine George Brain's whereabouts official opinion was forced to consider the possibility that the hunted man could have committed suicide.

I remember being personally caught up in the excitement of the manhunt, for the Features Editor of the London *Evening News* rang me up in the middle of that dragging week in July and asked me to let him have at very short notice two thousand words to be headed, "What it Means to be On the Run," with special reference to the vast manhunt then being carried out to discover the whereabouts of George Brain, the most wanted man in Britain.

It was a curious coincidence that brought an abrupt end to

the manhunt, the kind of coincidence that occurs more frequently in real life than most people realise, and one that most crime novelists could not afford to employ without inviting harsh criticism.

During that last week of July a pair of sharp eyes in the head of a schoolboy found George Brain, and the schoolboy was on holiday with his family, who lived in—Richmond. In short, it was a boy from Brain's own area of London who found the wanted man lying holed up like an animal under a cliff on the Isle of Sheppey, in the Thames Estuary.

Not only that, but the boy knew Brain by sight!

The boy's family were staying near Sheerness, and on the day of his momentous discovery the lad went for a ramble along the weedy beach near the tall Minster Cliffs. There was a good deal of brushwood covering the chalk cliffs, decorated with bright clumps of gorse and broom, and it was movement among the bushes that caught the boy's sharp eye.

He saw a bearded figure with his clothes in rags, his hair matted, staring at him for a moment before the wild-looking apparition vanished. But that curious momentary confrontation alerted the boy to the fact that he was looking at the suntanned and bearded face of someone he recognised.

The boy turned around and ran back the way he had come to break his news to his father, who, once he was sure his son was not mistaken, set out to inform the Sheerness police. A search party was collected and started out for the Minster Cliffs.

Brain was found not where the boy had seen him, but hidden among the bushes growing out of the cliff face about half-way down. Two constables began to climb towards him. It was hot work in the full glare of the sun, but when they came up with the bearded man he took no immediate notice of their intrusion. In its way, this was a piece of inverted bravado. George Brain, the uncouth and dirty-looking character who had been living rough for more than a week, and who was suspected of having murdered a woman for her money and of dumping her body in a lovers' lane, was found pouring over the printed pages of a paperback novel entitled *The Island Lovers.*

There was not only coincidence in the finding and taking into custody of George Brain, but there was also a good deal of irony.

The fugitive was brought back to London after Inspector Henry had gone to Sheerness to collect him. When charged formally with Rose Atkins' murder he said, "I'll speak the truth. It's the best way."

Not every lawyer in the country would agree with such a naive assertion from a prisoner so recently charged with a capital crime. But in the generation that has elapsed since George Brain's arrest the members of the general public have become much more sophisticated and cynical in their attitude towards the police and towards what they believe are their own rights as citizens under the law. So much so that a centuries-old principle has given way under the weight of awareness, and the unanimous verdict of a jury has been recommended to be replaced by a majority verdict.

But when George Brain made his formal statment to the police after being charged his neck was in jeopardy and it would require the unanimous verdict of a jury to free it or break it according to legal ritual.

His statement, however, revealed that in the past nine days George had used his brain to discover the difference between murder and manslaughter, and his avowed readiness to tell the truth must be accepted in the light of his more personal cogitations between spells of reading *The Island Lovers.*

It read:

"I met the girl several months ago. I have seen her about four times altogether. I knew her as Rose. On the Wednesday night I just picked her up at the corner of the road. She was sitting in the van next to me. She said, 'I am in financial difficulties and I want some money.' I said, 'You will not get much out of me.' She then said, 'I'll report you to your firm about your van being out late if you don't give me some money.' I said, 'Don't be silly'."

He must have followed the dialogue of *The Island Lovers* with close attention for its dramatic impact. The statement continued:

"She knew my name was George Brain, as she had seen my driving licence. I then struck her with my hand. She started screaming. Then everything seemed to go blank, and I hit her with the starting handle which I kept in the van. I know I got a cut on the ring finger of my right hand. When I came to there was her body lying in the van. I then drove down the road and turned towards what I thought was the right, and then lifted her body out to the side of the road. I drove straight home. Mum and Dad were up and Mum asked where I had been. I told her that I had trouble with the motor.

"When I got up next morning I threw some water on the inside of the van to wash the blood out of it. I then drove away and picked up Frost and went to work. I gave the van a good wash when I got to work and then put the rags in a bag, poured petrol over it, and burned it in the dust-bin.

"I opened the girl's handbag. There was about four shillings in it. I took this out and then hid the handbag. I had a snob's knife in the van. I hid it on an iron beam in the garage. The knife was bloodstained, but it had been with the rags. I took about thirty pounds of the firm's money. I told the girls in the office that I had left the money at home. Instead, I went to the dogs at Wimbledon, betting, and lost the lot."

The knife left in the garage had been found by the police and the blood on it tested. It was of the same group as Rose Atkins'. The burned rags had been examined by Dr. Roche Lynch, the Home Office analyst. But the statement, while mentioning these discoveries, omitted reference to the stab wounds on the murdered woman and to the tyre marks on her stocking. So it was a calculated statement. George Brain, in short, was not so naive as he had wished to appear in Sheerness police station when Henry had cautioned him.

Moreover, he had referred to the four shillings found in Rose Atkins' handbag, but had omitted knowing of a secret pocket in her fur and her custom of carrying money with her. It could have been that he had known of her habit of having the fur's pocket well lined, and had attacked her for what he thought the pocket contained.

Only to draw a terrible blank.

A murder for four shillings!

Murder, not manslaughter as his statement hinted. For there could only have been a very short time lapse between her taking a seat beside him in the green van and being struck with the starting handle, as Fred Cherrill had diagnosed in that early examination of the battered woman's head. Indeed, it could have been that Brain had used his own motive for money-seeking to suggest a reason for attacking her by claiming she had demanded money from him under a threat of possibly losing him his job.

There was another factor not cleared up by the statement. The frankly hackneyed claim of everything seeming to go blank was not supported by another piece of evidence. Irish Rose had struggled with her killer, and he had been aware of her struggling. He provided proof of this shortly after he had been arrested, when he was asked to account for four small scars on the middle finger of his left hand.

"That's where she bit me," he said.

Fred Cherrill was supplied with samples of the prisoner's fingerprints.

"On comparing them with the mark on Rose Atkins' handbag," the Yard man reported afterwards, "I found that it corresponded with that of the prisoner's right forefinger. Nor was my evidence challenged on this point."

The murder interrupted a romance and a planned wedding. On the Friday evening before Brain decamped he called on his fiancée and she noted nothing unusual in his appearance or manner, possibly because her mind was filled with details for their forthcoming wedding in the following week.

But Brain was not a man given to fretting long about his misdeeds. So perhaps it was not surprising that his fiancée observed no overt change in him or any sign of preoccupation or nervous tension. Indeed, Jack Henry has explained how, after his arrest, Brain appeared somewhat nonplussed, but, as the Yard detective said, "That was the only time I ever saw him show the slightest trace of emotion or remorse. Afterwards he was never otherwise than smiling, jaunty, and apparently carefree."

He was not even stricken by the outcome of his trial at the Old Bailey, and appeared throughout what would have been an ordeal to most men curiously detached and aloof from the significance of the dire proceedings. For hours he seemed to be dozing in the dock. This almost callous attitude towards his own fate can be compared with another incident recorded by the man who arrested him.

It was Inspector Henry who drove Brain to the police court for his first appearance before a bench of magistrates to hear the case that could be made out against him. On the way to the court Brain turned to Henry and asked him to turn up the window. Henry looked at him in some surprise, for it was a warm summer's day.

Brain winked at him.

"I mustn't get a draught in my neck, must I?" he grinned.

The Old Bailey jury who heard the case of George Brain argued pro and con were only absent from their seats fifteen minutes before returning with a verdict of guilty. After being sentenced the prisoner turned from the dock towards the steps leading down to the cells below the Central Criminal Court.

"So I am to be hanged by the neck, am I?" he was overhead to mutter, as though debating the fact objectively with himself.

Yet there was a final irony to be recounted before he stood with studied indifference on the gallows trap. He had killed a woman suffering from an incurable disease. His victim would have been dead in less than a year if she had never accepted a lift from the driver of a green Morris Eight van on a sultry night in July.

2

THE CASE OF THE DEVIL'S HOLE

SUPERINTENDENT John Wilson Murray, who became chief of the Criminal Investigation Department of the Province of Ontario, was one of the greatest manhunters Canada, home of the justly famed Royal Canadian Mounted Police, had produced in a century of independent nationhood. In fact, if Expo 67, the great Canadian exhibition in Montreal to mark the passing of that memorable century, had had a single exhibit devoted to the world's great police manhunters the host nation could hardly have done better than be represented by Murray.

The Old Fox some of his contemporaries called him. He earned the nickname because few criminals could out-smart him. But his record contains a number of great cases where he had little luck but plenty of hard work. He was a man who never depended on luck, and one who could work the clock round. Often in his career that was just as well.

He had to work long hours on the case that is perhaps best associated with his work internationally. To Murray it became known as the Case of the Devil's Hole. It was equally a devil of a case.

For Murray it began in the long-ago winter of 1889-90, which was a bad one in Southern Ontario. The temperature dropped well below zero and stayed there for months. At that time there was a wide expanse of waste extending for upwards of fifty miles which was a desolate place about which strange tales were told. It was called locally the Blenheim Swamp, and in summer, when the frozen waste had thawed out and the shrubs and brush had taken on new green, it was a place that was colonised by undesirables from the towns, by men on the run from the police, by tramps who had reason to lie concealed after dropping from the freight cars that crossed the lonely expanse of derelict land.

In the summer months the hobo colony made their headquarters in the very heart of the unsavoury swamp, at a place called the Devil's Hole. Rumour claimed it had been the scene of much violence and that the bodies of men who had died were concealed under the dark earth.

The place was even claimed to be haunted.

In winter it might well have been, for when the earth was frozen the whole swamp was deserted, and the Devil's Hole was a lost region in the ironbound earth. No hobo, however hardy, could live through the rigours of the swamp in mid-winter. By late February, in any normal year, the swamp had been deserted by humans for more than four months.

The first to penetrate the swamp in late February 1890 were a couple of woodsmen from the small town of Princeton. The date was actually February 22nd.

That was a date John Wilson Murray remembered for the remainder of his life.

The two woodsmen were approaching the Devil's Hole, in the heart of the swamp, when suddenly one of them stopped in his tracks and caught at his companion's arm.

"A body!" he exclaimed.

The second man looked to where the first was pointing. He too saw the huddled figure lying face down on the frozen ground. The two men broke into a run. Minutes later they were hurrying back the way they had come to report a murder. There could be no doubt on that point, at least.

The young man whose body they had come upon had been shot in the back of the head. Twice.

Moreover, he was no one they knew. Which meant that he was a stranger to the swamp.

The police went out and collected the body and brought it back through the swamp to Princeton, where it was examined by a doctor and the local police chief. A report was made out, including the details of how the body had come to be found, as well as the fact that the dead man was about twenty-one years of age and had been wearing good-quality clothes that were of obvious English cut and style. There was little else in the report, for in the dead man's clothes was found no paper of any kind by which he could be identified. In fact, nothing had been left in his pockets, and a tailor's label had been ripped from inside his coat, while laundry markings had been cut from his undergarments.

It looked as though whoever had pulled a trigger twice to ensure the young man's death had been very deliberate in choosing a place for disposing of the victim and had been equally deliberate in trying to ensure that the dead man's identity would not be discovered.

There was a formal inquest. The jury returned a nominal verdict of murder against some person or persons unknown, which meant that a case of murder was handed back to the police.

A report of the inquest appeared in a few Canadian papers, but it rated no large headlines. Denizens of the Devil's Hole rarely found their names in print even when they were alive. This one was dead and had no name.

Most newspaper readers could have missed the few lines reporting the woodsmen's find if their glance that day was casual. But one man whose glance was anything but casual was Murray's. The Princeton report had arrived on his deask, and the Ontario C.I.D. had a new murder case on its files.

Murray, as has been pointed out elsewhere, was born in Scotland. He was a contemporary of Allen Pinkerton, another

Scot, and matched his fellow-Scot in height and breadth of shoulder, for both men were over six feet and of sturdy build. Indeed, up to a point, the police careers of the two great detectives had run on parallel lines, as other writers have noted. Both had become involved in the American Civil War, and both had spent a significant part of his career engaged on Secret Service work. But whereas Pinkerton went on to further the activities and establish the reputation of the famous firm of private detectives he had founded in Chicago, Murray went north across the Canadian border and took up detective work in a neighbouring province until he was chief of its C.I.D.

From his Toronto office John Wilson Murray, who had also worked as a railroad detective in Canada, organised a team of plain-clothes men who were unquestionably the best detectives in Canada in their time.

It was when they learned that the riddle of the corpse found at the Devil's Hole had been handed to Murray to solve that reporters became really interested in the case. They assembled at police headquarters in Toronto to collect a statement from the C.I.D. chief.

"There's little I can tell you," Murray said grimly, but with his well-known air of supreme confidence, "except that we'll find the killer."

"Who's the dead man?" a reporter asked.

"That's another thing we'll find out," Murray added, keeping a straight face.

He went to Brantford, which was the nearest town of any size to the grim Blenheim Swamp. There he was confronted by reporters who had preceded him. Among them were some Americans, who, knowing Murray's reputation, had decided he might have something sensational to tell them.

Murray didn't disappoint them. Although he had no hard news to hand out he gave them a run-down of what he hoped to achieve.

"This is not a case of a man being set upon in some lonely spot and robbed," he told the gathered reporters. "I'm out to find a cold-blooded killer who deliberately planned how to murder someone and dispose of the body in a place where he could expect it would not be found until past identifying. Moreover, I am already certain that the victim came from a good-class family, possibly not even from this country."

That was enough to send Murray's audience, when the conference broke up, hurrying to Eastwood, at that time the nearest railway station and therefore the place from which they could dispatch Murray's words. Afterwards the reporters went back to learn the result of a visit Murray had made to the Devil's Hole with some of his city detectives.

As things turned out the examination of the place where the dead man had been found offered nothing to help Murray's inquiry, but it did start a suspicion in his mind. For instance, why should anyone be making for the Devil's Hole of all places? To Murray's searching mind the answer implied a knowledge of the Blenheim Swamp.

If that was the case, he might be able to narrow down his search quite considerably. It meant the murderer had deliberately led the victim to that place to shoot him. They must have walked.

Murray started a search of the most likely route taken by two men making from the direction of Eastwood. It was when he was tracing back that route that he came upon a most incongruous article for such a wild and deserted area. It was a somewhat fancy cigarette holder. Not only was it made of silver, with an amber mouthpiece, but it had three initials engraved on it. Obviously it was a possession of value, and perhaps of sentiment, to its owner. Not something that would be thrown away.

The initials were F.C.B.

Keeping to his own reasoning, Murray deduced that the cigarette holder must have belonged to the victim. The killer would have had no reason for discarding his own property. But the victim might have dropped the cigarette holder in a moment of heated argument, possibly while becoming suspicious of his companion's intentions. Alternatively the murderer could have tossed away an object that might help to identify the victim of his carefully prepared murder plan.

Back out of the dreary frozen swamp, the Ontario C.I.D. chief wired a number of shipping agencies in New York and also in Quebec. He asked them to check back and report the arrival of any passenger from Europe with the initials he had found on the fancy cigarette holder.

Formal descriptions of the dead man had been prepared by his staff, and these were passed on to the Press. The case of the unknown found shot twice at Devil's Hole at last began to be reported with headlines.

Murray depended on the general public's interest being kept alive by follow-up newspaper reports on the investigation, for he was in advance of his time in believing that the widest publicity helped a police inquiry rather than hindered it, and he invariably began a case believing that help could come from a member of the general public if sufficient interest was created in the human drama. Every passer-by in the street was a potential ally in a manhunt. Murray never overlooked that fact.

Within three days of the coroner's inquest closing with its murder verdict Murray had still to learn the victim's name, but the case was already receiving considerable attention in the United States as well as in Canada.

It was on the third day that a stranger walked into a Princeton hotel, took a room, and wrote his name in the register—John R. Birchall. Under the nationality column he wrote "Englishman." Mr. Birchall was not alone. He arrived at the hotel accompanied by a young woman with serene good looks whom he introduced as Mrs. Birchall. After installing himself and Mrs. Birchall in their room the newcomer came down and made a few inquiries.

All were about the Devil's Hole murder.

The next day he sought out Murray, who was back directing the purely local investigation.

"I think I may be able to help you," he told a genuinely surprised John Wilson Murray.

"I'd be grateful indeed for any help you can give me, Mr. Birchall," Murray said bluntly.

It looked as though the publicity he had encouraged was bringing results sooner than he had anticipated.

Birchall explained that he had only lately arrived in North America from England. But on the Atlantic crossing he had made the acquaintance of a young man who answered the descriptions he had read in the newspapers.

"I think it is just possible he may be the Devil's Hole victim," he told Murray.

He went on to explain that he and his wife were actually staying in Buffalo, in New York, and he had to return there. But as he had a few free days they had both come to Princeton to learn if the dead man could be the young passenger they had met coming out from England.

Murray was faced with a dilemma. The dead man had been buried after the closing of the coroner's inquest. There was only one way of discovering if Birchall could identify the victim. Murray took it.

He arranged with a local magistrate to have the body exhumed. This was done without any loss of time, and it was actually within hours of being told of the young passenger Birchall had met on an Atlantic crossing that the tall Englishman was accompanied to a bare room where the lid of a coffin had been removed to reveal the features and figure of the Devil's Hole victim.

Murray, however, did not look at the corpse in the coffin when the covering drape was removed. He was watching closely the face of John R. Birchall. He saw the look of horror that crossed it. Birchall started back a pace and gave a short exclamation. He turned his staring eyes and saw Murray watching him.

Birchall moved away.

"It's the young man I met on the way out," he confirmed.

"You'll remember his name, Mr. Birchall," Murray said quietly.

The other lost his look of horror, and frowned as he appeared to reflect. His frown deepened as he shook his head.

"I'm afraid I don't remember it. I'm sorry," he said with a shrug, and then appeared to reflect again. "However, I have a feeling that the name began with a B, like my own."

Murray asked a number of other questions, all calculated to stimulate the other man's memory, but Birchall insisted he could not recall the dead man's name.

Birchall offered profound apologies for not being more helpful, and went back to the hotel. The next day Murray called there to see him and was introduced to Mrs. Birchall.

"I've come," he told Birchall, "because it occurred to me that you might remember the dead man's initials."

Birchall seemed surprised by the request. He turned to his wife and put a question to her.

"I don't think we ever knew Fred's initials, did we, dear?"

Mrs. Birchall's blue eyes were very wide and her pretty mouth pouted a little as she shook her head slowly.

"His initials? No, I don't think we did, darling."

Murray was always sensitive to other people's reactions. Possibly because he had come to depend on them for telling him more than the persons themselves were aware.

He now had the impression that he was listening to a rehearsed piece of dialogue that did not necessarily ring true, though it was made to sound spontaneous. He felt, however, that this was not the moment to arouse the Birchalls' suspicions about his own motives.

Thanking them, he left the hotel.

The Birchalls professed not to know the initials of the dead man, whom they had known, yet they believed his surname began with a B and they had called him Fred, which meant they had been on somewhat intimate terms with a shipboard companion. Moreover, if Frederick was a first name, then he had two initials out of three. F.B. from F.C.B. left that middle C.

Murray left the hotel and began an inquiry into the comings and goings of the Birchalls since they had arrived in Princeton. He learned something he found of more than passing interest. Birchall had claimed they would be returning to Buffalo. But Murray discovered that the Englishman had already arranged to travel to Hamilton.

Murray wired the Hamilton police. He asked for the Birchalls to be watched day and night when they arrived from Princeton and not to be allowed to return across the border to the U.S.A.

A further outcome of the inquiry about the Birchalls in Princeton was a few jogged memories. Murray learned from one or two persons that they had a feeling they had seen John R. Birchall previously at some time. It took a good deal of patient inquiry to run down what the feeling really amounted to, but apparently Birchall was the double of a man who had stayed in Princeton a couple of years before.

"Who was the man?" Murray wanted to know. "Was he another Englishman?"

The reply he shook loose surprised him.

"He was an earl of something," he was told. "Called himself Lord Somerset."

This self-proclaimed peer had, he learned further, stayed at Woodstock, which was not a great distance away. He had arrived and been seen around the district, and had been pleasant enough to those he spoke to, but suddenly he had left, and after his departure he had been forgotten.

Until Murray began asking about the Birchalls.

Murray drafted a cable to Scotland Yard. It contained two descriptions, one of the man found at Devil's Hole, the other of John R. Birchall. He wanted anything the Yard could discover about either.

He was surprised by the reply he received from London.

It informed him that inquiries had established that a Mr. and Mrs. John Reginald Birchall were currently known to be travelling in the United States and Canada.

Birchall, who had been to Oxford, was understood to be a man of private means. His family were believed to be of good standing. The reply added the information that Mr. and Mrs. J. R. Birchall were said to be in the New World with a pair of young male companions who were in the nature of being their protégés. It was an arrangement made as the outcome of an advertisement Birchall had made. He had inserted the following in several London papers:

"Canada. University man having a farm wishes to meet gentleman's son to live with him and learn the business, with view to partnership; must invest £500 to extend stock. Board, lodging, and 5 per cent interest till partnership arranged. Address: J. R. Birchall, Primrose Club, 4 Park Place, St. James's, London."

Scotland Yard's surprising news concluded with the information that the two travelling companions with the Birchalls were both young men who had paid the advertised premium of five hundred pounds each to learn farming in Canada on the farm Birchall claimed to own in Southern Ontario. The names of the young men were F. C. Benwell and Pelly.

When he had finished reading the Yard's cable Murray knew the name of the Devil's Hole victim.

F. C. Benwell—Fred.

Without loss of time he contacted the Quebec shipping agents again, but none was able to give him news of such a quartet arriving from England. Murray sent the same request to agents in New York, and after a short interval received the news he wanted. The Birchalls and their companions had not, apparently, journeyed to Canada. They had crossed to the United States.

Murray believed he knew why.

To make tracing their movements more difficult if that were ever undertaken.

The Ontario C.I.D. chief now required confirmation and enlargement of what he had learned. He cabled Benwell's parents, requesting details of the arrangement made by their son with John R. Birchall.

Benwell's father replied without delay. He told Murray that his son Frederick had answered Birchall's advertisement, had met him by appointment, and he had paid the required premium of five hundred pounds to entitle him to learn how to farm in Canada on Birchall's extensive farm, which was in Ontario.

The news, of course, was what Murray expected. But now he had hard facts to replace deductions and an occasional piece of guesswork. He knew that both Benwell and Pelly had been cheated in a coldly calculated con game. But not by an average type of con man, who was out solely for a profit and a chance to vanish with it.

Birchall was greedy. He wanted his profit and he wanted the victim to vanish. It was rather like eating his cake and still having it.

However, this assessment placed Birchall in a unique category as a killer. He was a clever schemer. He thought in terms of finalising what he undertook, and he had nerve. A man without nerve would not have arrived in Princeton and sought an interview with the chief detective trying to find him.

But Murray realised that Birchall's nerve was also a weakness that could contribute to his being unmasked for the scheming killer he was. It was more than curiosity that had driven Birchall back to the neighbourhood of the crime. He had been unable to stop himself from wanting to know what the authorities were doing, and he had sought to throw dust in Murray's eyes by professing to help him.

There remained Pelly.

What had become of the second young male companion of the Birchalls? Neither Birchall nor his wife had referred to Pelly. Could the reason be that he was dead?

It was a possibility Murray had to face. Had Birchall killed two young men for a thousand pounds?

He started a new investigation to find out by directing inquiries to the police in Buffalo and at the same time checking that Birchall owned no farm or any land at all in Ontario. The American reply was not delayed. Murray was informed that the Birchalls had booked in at a Buffalo hotel on February 16th. They had remained there until they had journeyed north into Canada.

His next piece of helpful news came from nearer to hand. It was indirectly the outcome of the inquiry to establish that Birchall owned no farmland in the province. A girl who lived in one of the small country towns along the Grand Trunk railroad which skirted the north of Blenheim Swamp had recalled seeing two strangers that were walking in the direction of the swamp.

That was on February 19, in the early morning.

Murray lost no time in visiting the girl, who was fifteen and not too happy at having drawn upon herself the attention of detectives from Toronto. But Murray took his time to allay the girl's fears and when he left was certain that his new witness had seen Benwell going to his death with his murderer.

"Did either of the two men see you?" Murray had asked.

"No," she had told him, very positively.

She had been equally positive about the younger man being in a happy frame of mind, for he had appeared to be laughing and joking with his older companion. She agreed both men had been well dressed by Ontario country standards.

But equally important was her last admission to Murray before he left.

"An hour later I saw one of them walking back from the swamp. He was the older man. The younger man was no longer with him."

According to the medical evidence the Devil's Hole victim could have been shot any time up to four days before he was found, depending on the severity of the night frosts in that region of the swamp.

Murray was now convinced that Benwell had ended up in the swamp because his killer was not unfamiliar with the region. This turned his attention back to the self-proclaimed Lord Somerset and the peer's likeness to Birchall. If Lord Somerset had been Birchall using an assumed title, then Birchall's familiarity with the district was explained, also his readiness to refer to property in Ontario when advertising.

He had his men check on the girl's claim, and one of them came upon another useful witness, a man who lived not a great distance from Eastwood who claimed to have heard a couple of closely spaced shots fired somewhere on the swamp on the morning of the 19th.

The times were checked. The shots had been heard about half an hour before the girl saw Birchall returning from he swamp alone.

The shots heard by the new witness could have been those that killed Benwell.

Murray had questions asked at Eastwood station about the morning of the 19th. The stationmaster now recalled that, on that morning, the train from Dundas was late due to the exceptional cold. It had made a connection with another train from Welland and Hamilton that had come on from Buffalo. He also recalled two men getting off the train when it finally arrived.

One was a good deal younger than the other, and it was the younger man who had an unusual cigarette holder in his mouth, which he dropped as they gave up their tickets. The stationmaster had picked it up.

He described the fancy cigarette holder found in the swamp, but did not remember the initials engraved in the metal. On the other hand he recalled meeting Lord Somerset two years before, and he waxed enthusiastic about Lady Somerset's genteel good looks. He described Mr. and Mrs. Birchall, who by this time had arrived in Hamilton.

Murray wired the Hamilton police to arrest the pair. He then started for Hamilton, where he found, to his amazement, not only the Birchalls in custody, but also a young man named Pelly awaiting his arrival. Pelly had come from Montreal.

The young Englishman told Murray how he had replied to the Birchall advertisement and agreed to pay five hundred pounds and go to Canada against his father's advice and wishes. He had joined the Birchalls and Benwell on a White Star liner leaving for New York. The four had journeyed from New York to Buffalo, where Birchall suddenly said he was going with Benwell to complete some private business and would be away a few days. He had returned on the 20th alone, saying that Benwell had been anxious to go on to the farm, and then announced that he was arranging to go and see Niagara by moonlight, a sight he had long promised himself. He invited Pelly to join him.

So the two men had started for Niagara, leaving Mrs. Birchall at the hotel. At Niagara, while overlooking the moonlit giant fall, Birchall had stumbled against Pelly and almost pitched the younger man into the maelstrom of foaming water hundreds of feet below.

"I knew then," Pelly told Murray, "that he was prepared to murder me."

As soon as he arrived back in Buffalo the Englishman packed his bag and left for the station, where he had caught a train to Montreal, without bidding his strange hosts good-bye. He had decided his life was worth more than the five hundred pounds he had lost by walking out on them.

When Murray saw Birchall he had his evidence arranged in damning order and read it over. Birchall denied it, whereupon Murray informed him that his wife would be charged with him. That broke Birchall's smooth reserve.

"My wife has never been a party to any of my plans," he told the Canadian detective. "She did not even know I had accepted those premiums. I must protest that your arresting her in this summary fashion is a monstrous outrage."

Fine words, but the man was shaken. Murray could see that. He decided not to go ahead with charging a woman who might win more sympathy in court than would help a prosecution's case. Ironically the trial was held at Woodstock, where the bogus Lord Somerset had stayed. There were reporters not only from American and Canadian newspapers, but also from English, French, German, and Italian. Indeed, so great was European interest in this sensational case that a direct cable connection was arranged between the court-house in Woodstock and a London office.

The trial lasted six days.

Each was both a production and an ordeal for the foppishly dressed man in the dock. The weather was cold, and over his London-tailored suit Birchall wore a heavy topcoat lined with fur. Despite his pleas the evidence built up by Murray proved incontestable, and the jury returned to announce that they had found John Reginald Birchall guilty of Benwell's murder.

He was sentenced to be hanged.

Strangely, it was exactly nine months since his landing in New York when Birchall walked to meet the hangman in Woodstock, on November 14th. In the two months that had passed since he had been sentenced he had been the recipient of many letters from women in both Canada and the United States who had been captivated by his well-dressed looks and posture during the trial. Some even offered marriage, and presumably they were serious. Others sent him red roses as a sign of a deep affection. It was all rather neurotic and unrestrained, and left the man who had known the quiet of Oxford's Brasenose not only cynical, but contemptuous.

On his way to fulfil his final obligation to the law he had flouted he was met by a tearful wife, and was allowed to embrace her. When she was taken from him by her sister John R. Birchall continued his short walk with body erect and head high.

For his wife's sake his last moments were lived in a manner that enabled the hangman to report, after loosening the gallows trap, "He died like a gentleman."

The great tragedy of John Reginald Birchall's life was that he was unable to live like one.

He was a cold and callous rogue without pity and with very little room for remorse in his educated make-up. The only benefit he bestowed on his family was dying more than three thousand miles away from them.

But it was many years before his grim notoriety was forgotten on both sides of the Atlantic. Yet there was just a chance that he might have got away with a double murder if Pelly had tumbled over the edge of a shaky parapet into Niagara's moonlit foam.

Because Pelly made off he felt he had to take the bull by the horns and confront Murray, who was still at Princeton. And he had less chance of fooling John Wilson Murray than he had of murdering the agile young Pelly.

But by the time he had found that out for himself it was too late to retreat. Murray himself had slammed the door of the escape route at Hamilton. That was where the case had ended abruptly, with Pelly's appearance.

However, to Murray must go the credit of having drawn Pelly into the open, prepared to testify against a man who had genuinely scared him. Murray and the Press had proved too much for Birchall's well-laid plans.

3

THE CASE OF THE BLACK DIARY

Some years ago when I was staying in Paris a journalist friend who had translated one of my books rang me up and asked me if I would like to meet Jean Belin, who had recently retired from the post of Commissioner of the Sûreté Nationale.

He said, "You mentioned Landru the other night when we were crossing the Rue de Rochechouart. Remember?"

I remembered very well. We had come down from the Square d'Anvers and crossed the Rue de Rochechouart on our way to have dinner with an editor. I had said, "Where is Number 76?" and had been asked why I was interested in the address. I had said the one word, "Landru."

"Where does Belin live?" I asked my friend, who was at that time a crime reporter on *Qui-Detective*.

"In Chennevières."

I knew it. A pleasant little town on the Marne to the east of Paris. Under an hour's run, allowing for the traffic in the Paris suburbs.

"Make it one afternoon this week," I said.

A couple of days later I drove with my journalist friend out past the Bois de Vincennes, and an hour later was seated in a pleasant garden with tall ironwork gates between leafy trees listening to a man who had been called the greatest detective in

France. He smoked a big-bowled pipe, and he had the sort of smile that gets lost among the genial wrinkles in a square face. In the top half of that face, under a square forehead, were a pair of twinkling eyes that could harden with the rapidity of molten metal plunged into ice-cold water.

I liked him, and I liked the laughing and most pleasant little woman who was Madame Belin. She kept us supplied with drinks throughout a very warm early September afternoon.

It was an afternoon I shall never forget. It was the afternoon I heard about Henri-Désiré Landru from the detective who was, in very truth, the mass murderer's doom.

At the close of the First World War Jean Belin returned from fighting his country's enemies to take up the war against the criminals in the capital. He joined the Sûreté Nationale, and was attached to the First Mobile Brigade. Its headquarters was then, as now, in the Rue des Saussaies, and Belin was given a desk in one of the building's many offices.

He remembered quite clearly the April day in 1919 when he found on that desk a file containing the known details about the disappearance of two women. The persons who had reported them as missing stated that they had last been heard from when at Gambais.

On that 6th of April, 1919, the place-name meant nothing to the man whose name, as a detective, was to become firmly associated with it in the annals of international crime. Gambais was less than forty miles from Paris. No main road ran through it. As a place it was rather off the map. So far as Belin was concerned, anyone who went to live there in 1919 had virtually disappeared.

Today, a half-century later, it remains a small place, inconspicuous among the farther environs of the French capital, but one remembered for the ill-repute of its Villa Ermitage.

In the file he went through Belin came upon the names of three men who were known to have been associated with the missing women, Buisson and Collomb, both around fifty, and each of the pair a widow.

The names of the trio of friendly males were Dupont, Cuchet, and Fremyet. The first-named was believed to have left for Rouen, but police inquiries in the city had not discovered his whereabouts.

It was little enough to go on, and the file contained nothing to suggest that the few facts contained in it would precipitate Jean Belin into his most famous case, one that would make his name remembered for the remainder of his life throughout France.

The person behind the inquiry into the whereabouts of the missing widows was Madame Buisson's sister, a Mademoiselle Lacoste. She had gone to the police some days before, asking them to find out where her sister Célestine had gone. Célestine had been engaged to M. Fremyet, who had taken her to Gambais. But there was no news of Célestine Buisson or her fiancé in Gambais, and Mademoiselle Lacoste was now pressing for further action.

It was, apparently, while the inquiry into what had become of Madame Buisson was being made that the police had turned up the additional case of the second widow, Madame Collomb. She had relatives who had been informed that she, too, had suddenly become a middle-aged fiancée. The man she had agreed to marry was M. Cuchet.

A note came down from Belin's chief while he was studying the file. The words were succinct and full of admonition.

"Immediate action required on the file passed to you."

Jean Belin was always a man who refused to dispute the logic of the assertion that the shortest distance between two points is a straight line. Madame Collomb's relatives, he saw, lived not very far away in Paris. He collected his coat and hat and paid them a visit.

They were surprised to see him, but ready to tell him that their missing relative had first met M. Cuchet through answering an advertisement in a daily newspaper. At the time she had written she addressed her reply to a M. Petit. A meeting was arranged, and M. Petit curiously told his new pen-friend, who believed he had marriage in mind, that he really preferred to be known as Cuchet.

There had been subsequent meetings, but while Madame Collomb had considered herself engaged to her Petit-Cuchet, her new fiancé had shown remarkable shyness in bringing himself to discuss plans for their marriage. Madame Collomb had certainly not been encouraged to throw up her work with a milliner in the Rue Lafayette. When she had accompanied her Petit-Cuchet on a holiday to Gambais she had been hopeful, according to her relations. However, when Belin arrived at the smart little hat-shop in the Rue Lafayette and interviewed the couple of elderly women who owned it he learned that Madame Collomb's hopes were soaring.

They had received a number of postcards from their employee and friend. The latest referred to a trip she was about to take across the Mediterranean.

"That must be to Algiers," said one of the elderly milliners.

"Did you ever see M. Cuchet?" Belin asked.

"Once," he was told. "He looked in and brought us a message from Madame Collomb. She hoped we were well, and she was preparing her trousseau."

"She must be married by now," said the other. "Strange, though, she did not write us about it."

Belin silently agreed. He asked if they could give him a description of M. Cuchet. Before he left the shop in the Rue Lafayette he had a fair idea of what Madame Collomb's new love looked like. There were at least a hundred thousand men in Paris the description could fit.

For thick dark beards were the fashion again after the war years. And M. Cuchet's was very thick.

Above M. Cuchet's very thick and very dark beard were a pair of penetratingly bright eyes, also dark, and above them a fine wide brow extending to a dome of hairless skull. M. Cuchet's baldness, seemingly, was offset by his bushy dark facial whiskers.

For the moment Jean Belin had progressed as far as he was able. He turned to Madame Buisson, the other missing widow. She had been engaged, according to her sister, Mademoiselle Lacoste, to a M. Fremyet, whom Belin traced to an address in the Boulevard Ney, where, according to the concierge, Madame Buisson had also stayed. Moreover, Fremyet had told the concierge that his fiancée had left to take a position helping in an American military canteen that was close by General Pershing's headquarters in France.

Like Madame Collomb, who might have gone to Algiers, Madame Buisson had vanished. Like M. Cuchet, M. Fremyet had departed.

Also like M. Cuchet, M. Fremyet had a bushy beard and was bald.

More than an idea was taking shape in Jean Belin's shrewd mind when he called on Mademoiselle Lacoste to ask some questions to which he hoped she would supply useful answers. But in this unlikely quarter he suffered a sharp reverse. Mademoiselle Lacoste refused to speak to him about her missing sister. He asked her why, and was given a strange answer.

She would only continue to discuss her sister with the detective she had first interviewed. He tried to change the woman's mind, but was unsuccessful. Mademoiselle Lacoste had strong likes and dislikes, it seemed, and Jean Belin came under the general heading of the latter.

He went back to his file and tried to get a line on the third masculine name in it—Dupont. He remained a very shadowy character in the background of the two women's lives until Belin established that Dupont, who had supposedly vanished in Rouen, also had a beard and was bald.

Three men, three names, one general appearance.

It would make a great deal more sense if all three were actually one man. There was more than the beard and the baldness to point to this. Cuchet had first called himself Petit. He had a habit of changing his name when he considered it advisable.

It was while studying the file again that he realised Mademoiselle Lacoste was known in Gambais, where she had gone to find news of her missing sister. Also, she had seen Fremyet. If he could induce her to return to Gambais she might be able to discover if the man had returned without warning him. Belin felt it was worth returning to interview the woman again and risk being snubbed a second time.

Actually, Mademoiselle Lacoste was angry at Belin's return.

"If you don't leave me alone I shall call a policeman," she threatened.

Belin was amazed. "I am a policeman, mademoiselle," he reminded her patiently.

"I don't believe you. I think you're an imposter, and I'm sure you're up to no good."

It seemed the woman was suspicious of any male after her sister had vanished with M. Fremyet.

"There is a simple way of making sure I am telling the truth," Belin told her. "Ring Inspector Adam, who works with me, at Sûreté headquarters. He will tell you I am working on this case. Will you do that?"

His insistence overcame her former scruples. She nodded and assured him she would do as he suggested.

"Good," Belin approved. "Then I want you to do something else. Take a trip some time soon to Gambais and find out if Fremyet is back. You know what he looks like. If you find out anything ring my office without delay."

The woman looked bemused, and Belin did not remain to watch the effect of his words wear off. He left and bought some lunch. He was still in his office at the Rue des Saussaies at seven that evening when the telephone on his desk rang. The police operator taking the call informed him there was a Mademoiselle Lacoste on the line and she sounded excited.

"Put her through," Belin said.

Mademoiselle Lacoste was, indeed, so full of her news that she could hardly speak coherently. But gradually Belin pieced together what she was telling him. She had been trying for more than an hour to reach him at Sûreté headquarters. She had seen Fremyet that same afternoon. Not in Gambais, but in Paris. Only a few hours after Belin had left her.

"Mademoiselle Lacoste," Belin said, "please don't leave your apartment. I am on my way to see you—now."

He hung up and once more returned to the address where he had been twice received with suspicion. This third time it was very different. Mademoiselle Lacoste was waiting for him to arrive at her front door. As soon as he was inside her apartment she was telling him how she had gone shopping a short while after he had left, which was about lunch time.

"I was in the Rue de Rivoli when I saw him," she ran on. "Oh, it was Fremyet all right. I'd know that beard and those eyes anywhere. And he was with another woman. Not my sister, you understand. Some strange woman, who was holding his arm and looking at him adoringly. It was quite nauseating."

Mademoiselle Lacoste was excited, incensed, and angry all at the same time. But she had more to tell. Because she had been both incensed and excited she had followed the pair to a large store and gone inside after them to the chinaware department. She told Belin she had hovered close by while Fremyet had chosen some china, and then taken a visiting card from his pocket and given it to the counter hand with a sum by way of deposit. Afterwards he and the strange woman had left the store and walked to a bus stop. Mademoiselle Lacoste had been just behind them when they boarded a bus that took them north to Montmartre, but she herself had been turned aside when about to get on the bus, which had been full.

So the exciting chase had ended at the bus stop. Fremyet or Cuchet or whatever he was now calling himself had got away.

"Do you think he might have noticed you?" Belin asked the woman.

Her reply shook him, it was so matter-of-fact.

"I don't see how he could have failed to recognise me," she told the Paris detective. "He looked straight at me."

If it was Fremyet, and if he had recognised Madame Buisson's sister, then he must have been alerted by the fact that he had observed her following him. Belin felt there was no time to be lost.

Despite the hour, he drove to the store where Fremyet had gone to the chinaware department. The place was closed for the night, but Belin found there was a watchman on duty, and from this man he obtained the address of the store's manager. He caught a taxi and drove to the far side of Paris, where he was in time to interrupt the manager just as the man was about to sit down with his wife to a late dinner.

The dinner was held back for a few minutes, and then Belin left. With him he had the address of the salesman who attended the chinaware counter. When Belin arrived at the man's home and explained what he wanted the salesman admitted that he recalled making the sale that afternoon very clearly. But he could not remember the bearded man's name.

"It is important that I have his name and address without delay," Belin told the salesman, who was quite ready to be helpful, and accompany the detective back to the store.

When they arrived he took Belin to the chinaware department and hunted through a drawer to find the visiting card reported by Mademoiselle Lacoste. It was a rather grubby piece of slim pasteboard on which was the printed name of Lucien Guillet, who described himself as an engineer.

Belin had expected the name would be a fresh one, and was neither surprised nor disappointed to find Petit-Cuchet-Fremyet —and possibly Dupont—running true to past form. He couldn't help wondering what the man's real name could be. It was certainly none of the string he had been told, and it was not Lucien Guillet, he was positive.

However, under this last alias the man of many whiskers, many women, and many names had provided an address.

76, Rue de Rochechouart.

Which, as Belin knew, explained the catching of a Montmartre bus travelling north from the city centre. The Rue de Rochechouart runs north from the Rue Lafayette to the Boulevard Rochechouart, in the heart of the Montmartre area. Remembering that Madame Buisson had worked in the milliner's in the Rue Lafayette, and that the bearded man had called on the two elderly milliners, Belin realised that the man he sought was keeping his activities limited for the present to a certain district he obviously knew well.

This may have been the outcome of over-confidence, which was a flaw in any man's character. Had the man changed his living habits, and with them the district in which he lived, he would not have been seen by Mademoiselle Lacoste.

Belin also realised that, if the man had indeed recognised her, as she believed, then he might have only a short while before his quarry did change his habits and his address, and he would be lost in the French capital.

He just might shave off his beard.

It was a possibility fraught with danger for a detective anxious to ask a great many questions of a man who obviously had a good many to answer.

By the time Belin had that visiting card in his pocket it was in the early hours of the next day, for apparently it had been found in the wrong drawer, and a good deal of time had been taken up finding where it had been mislaid. The detective caught a late-cruising cab and was driven to the Rue de Rochechouart.

No. 76 was an apartment house. At that hour he could not begin waking people to discover in which apartment resided M. Guillet. Furthermore, he could not enter the Guillet apartment in the middle of the night. French law forbade such an invasion of a private citizen's home at that hour. On the other hand, he was determined not to let this M. Guillet escape when daylight brightened the streets. So Jean Belin spent four hours propping up a wall near the entrance to the apartment house, smoking his pipe, and forcing his eyes not to close. They were some of the slowest hours he ever lived through. But at last daylight polished the sky over the Paris streets, and both officially and technically he was entitled to behave like a detective with business on the enclosed premises of No. 76.

He then rang the bell for the concierge, who appeared grumbling and was in no better frame of mind when told the caller was from the police. Indeed, the concierge only perked up when Belin mentioned Guillet.

The concierge told him that Lucien Guillet had left for the country the night before. With Guillet had gone his fiancée, Fernande Segret.

"They took plenty of luggage," the concierge informed the detective who had wasted a most uncomfortable night.

"Any idea when they'll be back?" Belin asked.

"They'll be away a week at least, I should say."

While the rest of Paris was rising from a night's sleep Belin made his way back to Sûreté headquarters, where he shaved before going out to get some breakfast. A few hours later he made a report to his superior in the department.

His chief's comment was far from encouraging.

"Just a wasted night, I'd say, Belin."

However, Jean Belin didn't see it that way. He was convinced that the vanishing Guillet was the same man as had advertised to meet a female and had become engaged to Madame Collomb, the same man who had met Madame Buisson. Two women had vanished and both had known him under different names. Now he had a new name and a new fiancée. As Belin saw it, there could be nothing coincidental in this. Everything about the man and his movements was deliberate, planned. Further, Mademoiselle Lacoste was right.

He had indeed recognised her and had left Paris within a few hours.

Belin thought of Gambais. Had Guillet gone there? He could not risk leaving Paris to find out, much as he was tempted to do so by his chief's lack of enthusiasm. If he went to Gambais the man could return to Paris and Belin might miss him. To avoid standing still on the case, quite literally, while watching No. 76 Rue de Rochechouart throughout one rainy day after another, he requested a warrant to be made out in the name of Fremyet. With this he would be empowered to make an arrest in order to question the arrested man.

They were sad, dreary days Belin spent hanging about the pavements of the Rue de Rochechouart. His only positive gain was the friendship of the concierge at No. 76, whose reserve broke down as the days passed, sufficiently, at any rate, for him to accept the beers Belin bought him in a nearby bistro. Over their glasses Belin heard of the bearded M. Guillet's astonishing success with the other sex.

That was something Belin did not doubt. Unfortunately the concierge could tell him nothing of the outcome of M. Guillet's whirlwind love affairs.

The week had almost passed, and it was coming up to midnight on the Friday as Belin sat alone at a window in a bar from which he could see a street-lamp on the far side of the road. The door of the bar opened, and Belin looked round and saw the concierge coming towards him. From the expression on the man's face he had news.

He bent towards Belin, with one hand on the back of the detective's chair, and said in a conspiratorial whisper, "He's back."

"Guillet?"

The concierge nodded.

"Alone?"

This time the concierge shook his head. "No, she's come back with him."

"Sit down," Belin said. He rose and collected two fresh glasses of beer. "All right if I come back with you and wait in your room downstairs? I don't want to miss him if he slips out."

The concierge took a deep pull at his beer before agreeing.

The pair finished their beers and went down the street to No. 76, and Belin waited in the concierge's small parlour until most of the occupants of the apartments had come in and retired. That was when he rose.

"I'll wait in the hall and let you get to bed," he told the concierge.

"You can wait in here," the other offered.

"Thanks, but if I dozed off he might slip out. I can't risk it."

So the concierge went to his bed and Belin took up another lonely vigil at the foot of the stairs. The time dragged, but not so heavily this time, for Belin was buoyed up with expectancy. It is doubtful if the concierge had much sleep, for he was up and about as soon as dawn had broken.

"I want you to go to the Rue de Saussaies for me," Belin told him. "Come back with another detective."

When the man had put on his coat and hat Belin moved nearer to the street door and took from his pocket a newspaper advertisement he had come upon during his patient wait. The advertisement offered a car, and the name of the man who owned it was Guillet.

It was all the pretext Belin required to go knocking on Lucien Guillet's door.

The concierge and another Sûreté detective returned, and Belin waited until nine-thirty before going up to the Guillet apartment and knocking on the door, which was opened by a not very stocky man of medium height who was dressed in pyjamas. Above them his face was masked by a bushy dark beard which jutted somewhat aggressively from his chin.

"What do you want?" he asked his callers suspiciously.

"I've come about the car at Etampes," Belin said.

The next instant the pyjama-clad figure was trying to shut the door, but Belin's foot was over the threshold and the two detectives forced the bearded man inside. The door went slamming back against the wall, and a woman's voice cried out in alarm.

Belin took out the warrant for the arrest of a man named Fremyet. But he carefully held it far enough from the bearded man's face so that he could not read the name written down.

"You'd better get your clothes on. I want you to come to Sûreté headquarters to answer some questions, monsieur," Belin said.

His glance passed beyond the man in pyjamas to the bed across the room. Belin's first glimpse of the almost naked Fernande Segret was of the woman lying prone in a faint.

The bearded man took his time dressing, but by the time he was ready to leave a gendarme had been summoned, and the other detective and the gendarme left with the bearded man between them.

Belin started to search the apartment, watched by a glaring and resentful Mademoiselle Segret. In the pocket of a jacket hanging in the wardrobe the Sûreté man came upon an envelope on which was written the name "Landru." He showed it to the woman, who shrugged her shapely shoulders and said it meant nothing to her. Which might be the truth, or might not. There was nothing else in the apartment to interest Belin.

He went out and joined his colleague and the gendarme with their prisoner.

"I stopped him from trying to get rid of this," said the other detective, handing Belin a small black diary that had been used as a notebook. "It's full of women's names."

It was indeed. That black notebook was to become notorious as Landru's *carnet noir*. In it was a complete list of his plans for dealing with the many women who had fallen for his dark blandishments. When he was searched a smaller pocket-book was found in a pocket of his coat. In this was written the names of Célestine Buisson and Madame Collomb, with another 273 names of women!

It was not long before Belin knew that his prisoner's real name was Henri-Désiré Landru, that he had been born in Verdun fifty-two years previously. He had a police record and had been charged at various times with eight cases of theft, forgery, and false pretences and duly sentenced. He was still wanted under his own name for an old crime committed in the year the war had broken out. The police file photo of Landru showed Guillet.

Between the pages of the black notebook Landru had tried to lose at the time of his arrest was a folded receipt. It was for the rent of a disused stable. Belin arrived at the stable to find it filled with furniture and clothes that had belonged to the many women Landru had become engaged to, and in that stable used as a store-room Belin found papers that had belonged to both Madame Buisson and Madame Collomb, as well as to four other women whose names were not known to the detective. When he checked he discovered that all four were reported as missing from their homes.

The next day after the arrest was a Sunday. Before midday Belin had arrived at the Villa Ermitage at Gambais. It was a lonely house, actually outside the village, and near a churchyard. Belin began a search. On a table he found a heap of love letters couched in extravagant terms of endearment. All awaited posting to different women. In the kitchen was a smelly stove coated with grease. In the days following Belin proved that since 1915 scores of women had been courted by Landu, who, after getting his hands on their possessions, had lured them to his Gambais villa, which he had taken in the name of Dupont. Columns of smelly black smoke had risen from the villa's kitchen chimney as the black-bearded murderer disposed of his victims' bodies in the greasy stove.

But Landru had lived a triple existence. He had a wife and family in Paris, who believed he was a second-hand furniture dealer. Without his family suspecting, he had lived a second life as the destroyer of countless women who had trusted him. He had been known to them by at least fifteen names. In the name of Raymond Diard he was also the tenant of a house at Vernouillet, where, in 1915, a Madame Cuchet and her son mysteriously vanished. He took the name Cuchet to put in an advertisement which snared Madame Collomb.

The garden at the villa was sifted and quantities of bone fragment that were human were discovered. Buried in mounds of stove cinders were the metal clasps from many dresses.

The work begun that Sunday morning went on for two years and a half before it was completed. By that time it was known throughout the world that Jean Belin had captured a monster in human guise almost without parallel in the history of crime. There was not much not known about Henri-Désiré Landru by this time. Even his former claim to the police of having been born in Verdun was proved to be a lie. He was born in Paris, the son of a business man who had become deranged and killed himself in the Bois de Boulogne. It was in 1914 that Landru found he could exert a curious fascination over middle-aged women. He had lived at eleven different addresses in the French capital.

Yet his family insisted he was a devoted husband and father, and Fernande Segret, his last dupe, was so deeply attached to this man, who would have killed her and burned her body in the villa's stove if Belin had not arrested him, that she refused to appear in court as a witness against him.

"He was affectionate and he respected me," she told Belin bitterly as she looked accusingly at the detective. She seemed unperturbed by the fact that she was wearing what had been called in the Paris newspapers the "death ring," the engagement ring used nine times previously by Landru, or that, at the time of his arrest, a Jeanne Falque believed herself engaged to him.

The famous trial of the French bluebeard opened in November 1921 in the Versailles Assize Court. The charge was of murdering ten women and a boy. Throughout Landru tried to appear aloof from his surroundings. It was an impossible pose and it was impossibly maintained.

"I have nothing to say."

That was his constant stock reply to any question levelled

at him by the prosecution. The outcome of such a trial was inevitable. He was found guilty and sentenced to death.

By that time Jean Belin, the detective who had arrested him, was famous throughout France.

Three months later, at four o'clock in the morning of February 25th, 1922, Anatole Deibler arrived in Versailles with his guillotine, and hundreds of troops were brought out to guard the prisoner and his executioner.

Landru appeared, minus his famous bushy dark beard.

"It will please the ladies," had been his smiling quip.

He knelt under the guillotine and placed his head in the lunette to await the fall of the axe Deibler had sharpened specially for the occasion. The executioner touched a lever, the axe fell smoothly, and Deibler's assistant bundled headless torso and head into baskets which were pushed into a waiting horse-drawn van.

From the moment of Landru's appearance at the prison gates until the horses rattled their hooves against the Versailles cobbles as they moved away with their gruesome load only twenty-six seconds had passed.

"Did you see Landru without his beard?" I asked Jean Belin as we sat in the sunny garden at Chennevières.

He knew what I meant and shook his head as he drew on his pipe.

"No," he said, "I didn't go to Versailles that last morning. What would have been the point?"

4

THE CASE OF THE VILLA'S CORPSE

KATINA, a young Egyptian maid employed in the sumptuous home of Max Karam, knocked on his bedroom door and waited for the customary gruff call to enter. The master of that large home on the coast outside Alexandria was a Syrian and a merchant. In his lifetime Karam had made a great deal of wealth. He was proud of what he had achieved. He was proud of his lavish home, and he was also proud of his lovely wife. Perhaps he was most proud, in his Oriental heart, of being a British subject. Being British had tremendous advantages.

One of them he was never to know. It was the advantage of having competent British medico-legal minds tackle the problem imposed by one's murder.

But when Katina knocked for the second time on the door that problem was close to being discovered. The maid waited, and still receiving no reply knocked for a third time.

It was twenty minutes to nine. She turned the handle of the door and entered Max Karam's wide bedroom. A few feet inside the room she pulled up short and stared.

Her master appeared to be sitting by the side of the bed, and asleep. At least, it was almost a sitting position. His legs were thrust out before him, and he had one hand overlaying the other, almost in an attitude of prayer. His mouth was closed and he appeared to be pouting in his sleep, for his eyes were also closed.

But there was no movement. His thickset body did not move with his breathing. No sound came from those pouting lips. The maid stared in bewildered fascination, and then slowly the truth filled her with terror.

Her master was dead.

The creamy mosquito netting that had been torn from its rails over the bed and now was twined around the squatting man enveloped a corpse. Only death could explain the overturned commode which appeared to be propped up on the stretched-out legs. The lamp that normally stood on the commode had fallen to the floor some distance away.

If the suddenly frightened girl had doubts, or if the thought crossed her mind that Max Karam had been taken ill and had collapsed when trying to get out of bed, sight of the blood on his nightshirt resolved them. Stifling her fear, she tip-toed closer and put a timid hand to touch the seated corpse.

The flesh was cold.

She stooped to move a limb, but found it rigid.

She remained in her stooping position, her wide eyes staring at what appeared to be a brown scorch mark on the right sleeve of the nightshirt. It couldn't make sense to her mind in its upset state at the discovery.

She rose to her feet and screamed.

The sound stilled abruptly as she took herself in hand. She turned and hurried from the room. As she closed the door of that room of death behind her she began calling. Within minutes the local police were speeding to the large house by the Mediterranean.

The date was January 15th, 1923.

The Egyptian police, who had been trained by British officers, competently began an inquiry into a crime they quickly established as murder.

They found a drying pool of blood on the mattress of the bed with the ripped-away mosquito net, which was dappled with blood splotches and in places had similar scorch marks to that on the sleeve of the dead man's nightshirt. Only inches from the tacky pool of blood in the bed was a bunch of keys on a steel ring.

Max Karam's nightly habit had been to place that bunch of keys under his pillow. It had been a precaution he had taken for many years, for one of the keys on the ring opened the safe in his shore home. In that safe was normally kept a considerable sum in cash as well as some valuable pieces of jewellery.

However, when the key was turned in the safe's door both money and jewellery were in their accustomed places. The dead man had not been robbed. Indeed, if robbery had been the motive the murderer had gone empty-handed from the scene of his crime.

The dead man had been beaten about the head, although this had not been readily apparent at first glance. High on the head were lacerations running parallel to one another, and from their direction and position it seemed that Max Karam had been struck while confronting his killer.

The murder weapon had been dropped or thrown away. It had fallen between the reclining corpse and the bed. The iron bar was about eighteen inches long. More of Max Karam's tacky blood adhered to one end of it, like a repulsive jelly that was turning black.

However, although the safe had not been opened, it appeared that an attempt had been made to force open the door of a stout wooden cupboard. Jemmy marks had been made in the edge of the door, in an attempt to prise it open. But the lock had held, and the door had not been successfully forced.

That was the sum total of what the bedroom had to yield to the search by the police. It was, to say the least, puzzling. From the bedroom the police turned their attention to the other rooms in the large house where women could be heard crying softly. They found, on the ground floor, a door with a hole in it that was oval in shape, and easily recognised by professional police eyes. The hole was approximately six inches long by half that across, and had been made by drilling a number of much smaller holes with a brace and bit and then breaking loose from the door the central piece these holes had ringed.

The method was one used by professional burglars in the Near East.

Outside the door with the oval hole lay a small pile of sawdust and wood turnings on the floor. A few inches away was the serrated central piece of wood that had been tugged loose to allow the entry of a hand, which had reached the inside bolt. This had been secured in a wall slot and held in place by a short chain which ran through a steel ring. It was a strange contraption, but should have proved effective against mere force in opening the door.

To the police this appeared a most curious discovery. For the person who had cut out the piece of the door by using a brace and bit had known where to start drilling to be sure of being able, later, to reach the chain and the bolt. Obviously the culprit had known the position of the bolt and the ringed chain.

Such a person was no stranger to the household on the shore.

In support of this were the severed wires of the electric alarm system. The wires that ran to the alarm bell had been cut, although the wires had been cunningly concealed in the wall. Actually the electric wires had been cut on both sides of the house, so that even the bells in the kitchen had been put out of action.

This thorough job had been completed when the telephone line had been severed.

The police were immediately suspicious of such a complete attempt to deceive them, as they considered. Their reaction was to suspect some member of the dead man's household of having killed him and then having drilled the hole in the door and cut the telephone and electric bell wires to make it appear an outsider had forced an entry.

If the police theory required any support it was supplied by the fact that a night watchman was employed to watch over the household during the hours of darkness. The man had seen and heard nothing. This pointed to his movements being known.

After completing their search the police returned to the room where the tearful widow awaited them. She was no longer crying, but gave visible signs of being distressed. However, she endeavoured to compose herself sufficiently to answer their questions.

She explained that on the previous night her husband had given a dinner party to some friends. The party had ended about midnight, as near as she could remember. Her husband had seen his guests leave, and afterwards the night watchman had been told to go round and secure doors and windows in the usual custom. When her husband had turned to go up to his bedroom she had accompanied him.

"I remained in his bedroom for about half an hour," she explained to the police.

"How did he seem?" they asked her.

"He was very happy. He talked about the party, and said he had enjoyed his friends coming."

"Would you say he was in good spirits, Mrs. Karam?"

"Oh, yes, certainly," the widow said with no hesitation.

"Your husband did not appear to you like a man expecting trouble?"

"Trouble? Why, no. Why should he expect trouble?"

But the police were there to ask questions, not answer them. They continued until she explained how she had been kissed goodnight by her husband, and had then left his room to go to her own, which was along a passage and was separated from her husband's by two intervening rooms.

She went on to explain how, as was usual with her, she had

fallen asleep almost as soon as she had climbed into bed. That would have been shortly before one o'clock, as near as she could tell. Some time later she was roused by a sound like a thud, as though something weighty had fallen. She did not know where, though it had sounded in the house. She had remained listening for some time, and decided she must have been dreaming. She turned over, closed her eyes, and went to sleep again.

She had been wakened by Katina. That was about half-past six, her normal time for rising each morning.

"I thought I heard a noise in the middle of the night, like a thump, Katina," she said to the girl. "You didn't hear it, I suppose?"

To her surprise the girl had said, "Yes, madame, I heard a heavy thumping sound. I thought it must be a shutter banging in the wind."

"We'll go and see, Katina," the mistress told her maid.

She put on some clothes, and the two went downstairs to look around the ground floor. It was daylight and the night watchman had left. Her hurried examination of the downstairs rooms revealed nothing out of place, and Mrs. Karam had returned to her room.

She was in that wing of the house when later Katina's cry of alarm rang through the house.

The maid had a much better idea of the time the thud had sounded.

"It was about three o'clock," she told the police.

The other servants in the large house had nothing to tell which offered a clue or reason for the violence and apparent forceful entry. The night watchman was also questioned. He was scared, but apparently telling the truth when he insisted he had heard nothing and seen nothing that night.

Police making a thorough examination of the garden surrounding the large house came upon a gap among the iron spikes topping the boundary wall in a grim-looking chevaux de frise. The missing spike was found on the ground outside the wall, and apparently had been broken off by someone tugging at it. From below the space left by the missing spike, on the inside of the wall, ran footprints in the soft earth. They led straight to the house. Detectives took plaster casts of several of the prints in the soil. They were compared with the footprints made by the various members of the Karam household, but provided no matching pair.

The police found they had to do some rethinking, not necessarily to change their ideas, but certainly to include some additional possibilities.

Meantime the body of the murdered man was removed to a mortuary in the town, and there a post mortem was undertaken by a medical officer attached to the British Consulate in Alexandria. Max Karam, the British subject, was being given the final service attaching to his nationality.

The medical man was somewhat surprised to find the dead man, aged somewhere in his early forties, had been such a splendid physical specimen. Karam had been of powerful physique, not a man to be tackled lightly by an intruder wishing to overcome him by force.

But Karam had suffered a dual attack.

The three contused wounds already observed by the police were traced across the vertex, front to back, without the doctor finding that the skull had been fractured. But the powder burns on the right sleeve of the nightshirt and in the mosquito netting pointed to a gunshot and the wound was followed from a contused puncture below the left eyelid to an entry wound behind the right ear. The bullet which had been fired into the back of Karam's head in cowardly fashion had penetrated the brain.

Curiously there were no powder burns at the back of the head and the short hairs in the nape of the neck and around the ear did not have that distinctive burned-powder smell. The suggestion was that the bullet had been fired from some distance.

The cap of skull was dissected and removed from covering the holed brain, which had marked haemorrhage on its moist surface. The bullet's passage was clear. It had travelled at right angles to the surface of the skull, splintering the base of the skull with fissured fractures and damaging the sphenoid bone.

The medical man's forceps removed a couple of cartridge wads and a copper-covered bullet from their hole in the punctured brain.

It looked as though Max Karam had been shot dead.

Then why the superficial wounds caused by the iron bar that had been found close to the bed?

The local police, confronted by the results of the post mortem, admitted they were puzzled to account for what had been found, but still clung to their theory that the murder had been done by someone in the dead man's own household. At least, it was a theory that covered a majority of the known facts, though by no means all.

A discussion at the British Consulate resulted in a suggestion that the Alexandria police were not reluctant to avail themselves of—the case, as one of murder, was presented formally to the Medico-Legal Department at Cairo, which was staffed with British officers.

A fresh investigation started.

A new theory resulted from the new consideration of the known facts. Max Karam had not been killed by someone inside his household. The murderer had come from outside, and the killer had been no novice at forceful entry as the use of the brace and bit showed plainly enough.

Further, the British members of the Medico-Legal Department found no smear of fingerprints on surfaces that could be expected to retain them. This suggested the killer, or even possibly killers, wore gloves. In short, a professional job. This, too, was supported by a fresh examination of the blood-smeared iron bar that had been found in the bedroom. It was shaped like a conventional jemmy, with a tapering point at one end and a curved claw at the other for easy levering. It was likely to be the jemmy used unsuccessfully on the stout wooden cupboard.

The jemmy went under a microscope. Traces of brass and chalk were found in some of the irregularities in the metal's surface near the ends. The blood on it was tested, and found to be of the same group as Max Karam's. Fibrous particles adhering to the jemmy were proved to be of the same substance as the cream mosquito netting.

It was decided after the most careful consideration that the bullet must have been fired when the mosquito net was drawn, and with the gun held close to the netting. Further calculations suggested that Karam was not lying prone in his bed at the time of the shot, but was actually sitting upright, perhaps with his feet out of the bed and standing against the edge, but certainly swathed in the mosquito net, which had not been drawn back.

The calculations pointed specifically to the victim's right arm being raised to protect his head. In this way the nightshirt sleeve had been scorched together with the netting over his head.

But at the same time Karam must have been facing a person who had struck him with the jemmy from in front.

This clearly indicated one had attacked with a gun in the rear, another in front wielding the jemmy. Two murderers. The one behind had moved to shoot from the right.

This could mean a pair of known professional burglars, who had carefully acquired knowledge of how the household was run and of its security aspects. If this was so, it was well nigh certain that they had entered through the forced downstairs door, crossed the ground floor to the wide marble staircase, and then crept up to the first floor. They had done this without disturbing the night watchman.

On the first floor the staircase branched off in two directions, the first towards Max Karam's suite of rooms, and the second towards another suite occupied by Karam's brother and the latter's wife.

The bell wires from each suite had been severed.

Having established how the murder had been committed the detectives from the Medico-Legal Department turned their attention to why. They started with the safe which, presumably, had been the thieves' target—always supposing theft to be the true motive for the entry and the resultant murder.

It was a wall safe built into the small dressing-room that adjoined Mrs. Karam's bedroom. As no attempt had been made to force the safe, it was believed that the thieves must have known, among other details of the household arrangements, that Karam slept at night with his keys under his pillow. The procedure they had followed was likely, first, cutting the bell wires and telephone line, then stealing to Karam's room to try working the bunch of keys from under the sleeping man's head. Karam could be expected to be sleeping like a log after the late party.

But Karam had wakened and immediately turned on his attackers and was hit over the head by the man holding the jemmy. There had been no light in the room, and Karam had been a shadow entwined in the mosquito netting. Moreover, he had been a man of considerable strength. The blows had not stunned him. Whereupon the other man had shot him in the head.

The intruders then panicked completely and ran from the house.

At a conference the Alexandria police accepted both the theory and the tentative reconstruction of the crime. They began pulling in known professional burglars for questioning. At this point the widow came forward with an offer of two thousand pounds' reward for information that would lead to the arrest and conviction of the killers.

The result of this offer was for an army of persons to come forward with a host of suspicious suggestions which, in very few cases, withstood the first few shrewd questions.

Three weeks passed from the night of the murder, and then a

Frenchwoman of the paved streets who was known to her clientèle as Henriette called at a police station and said she had something to tell.

She said she had been living with a German. This man had another German friend named Ferid Merkel, but Henriette said she was sure this was not the man's rightful name. Merkel liked the bottle, and when he had imbibed enough he became talkative. She had heard him speaking to the German she lived with about a burglary he and another man had undertaken. Henriette, after listening for some time, realised Merkel was boasting about participating in the Karam killing.

When she read of the reward that had been offered she decided the time had come to think of herself.

"If Merkel finds out I've been to the police," she said earnestly, "he'll open me with a knife. I shall want protection as well as a reward."

She was told to go home and say nothing and act normally. Detectives then set out to examine Merkel's lodging, where he lived with another man, when it was unoccupied. The police searchers came away with some burglar's tools and a pair of well-worn gloves. Among the former were a brace and bit. Sent to the laboratory of the Medico-Legal Department, the bit was found to be of the same size as that which had made the drilled holes in the villa door. Particles of brown paint were found in the teeth of one of the files among the tools. This matched paint on the forced door. The fingers ends of the worn gloves were smeared with a chalky substance that was proved to be limestone of similar quality and texture as that with which some of the Karam villa's walls were lime-washed.

The detectives at the Merkel lodging came upon a blue serge suit, in the jacket pockets of which they found gritty particles of sand and limestone as well as some small wood chips, a piece of rusty iron and a piece of jagged glass, and a small piece of plaster.

The wood chips had been taken from the forced villa door as

comparison of grain and cutting shape revealed, and the small piece of plaster could possibly have come from the Karam home.

One of the more interesting articles discovered at the lodging was a visiting card with the name Klaus Chefer. It was with a morocco jewel case that was empty and some toothpicks that had been taken from the Petrograd Restaurant in Cairo. In a drawer were found two photographs. Both were of women. One bore the photographer's name—Robert Hanneman, Leipzig. This one had stains around the edges and small holes at the top, where a nail had held it on a wall. The other woman was older, and did not look Nordic. Her photograph had been taken at the London Studio, Cairo.

The laboratory of the Medico-Legal Department established that fair hairs taken from a brush and comb in the lodging had atrophied roots. This meant that the head those hairs had come from was going bald. On the other hand, hairs taken from a felt hat and from the collar of the blue serge jacket were much longer and almost black. But among the long dark hairs on the jacket collar was one fair hair of shoulder length—a woman's.

It didn't take the detectives long to discover that Merkel was short and stumpy and fair, going bald, and his fellow-lodger, whose real name was Klauss, was taller, with dark hair. Moreover, while Klaus Chefer was in fact Klauss, Ferid Merkel was actually a man named Doelitzsch.

Inquiries were made at the German Embassy and a very interesting story was told there of two German sailors who, on the last day of January, had reported meeting another German on the 18th in Alexandria. He had told them his name was Herman Klauss and he was living under the name of Klaus Chefer. He had invited them to visit him aboard the *Valtamery*, in Alexandria's harbour, and there he had boasted about a burglary he had done up the coast with another sailor named Merkel. The German visitors to the docked ship had been told details of the burglary that made them realise they were hearing about the crime at the Karam villa. They had talked over the position and decided to go to the German Embassy and report what they knew.

Unfortunately since then the *Valtamery* had sailed through the Suez Canal for India.

The Egyptian police were not slow in cabling the Indian police, and before long these cabled back that they were bringing a Magnus Klausen to Egypt. They arrived with their prisoner on April 13th, but he proved to be telling the truth when he said he was not Herman Klauss under another name. Incredibly, however, the Indian sergeant who had travelled with Klausen recognised the wanted Klauss, when shown the German's photo, as a man at that moment in jail in Calcutta. He had been arrested for jumping ship.

It took more weeks, but eventually Klauss was brought back to Egypt, by which time Merkel had been traced to a steamer that had sailed for Germany. One of the embassy secretaries had recognised the photograph of Merkel as that of a sailor named Fritz Doelitzsch who had signed on for the trip aboard the *Georgia*.

That was on January 29th, a week before Henriette had gone to the police.

The *Georgia* was traced to Trieste. The police there were wired by the Italian Consulate in Alexandria. The German Consulate in Alexandria also wired the German Consulate in Trieste. Within a few hours the wanted man was in custody and bound again for Egypt.

The next move in a sensational international case was by the German Embassy in Cairo. It claimed extra-territorial right to try the two arrested Germans under German law for a capital crime. This was duly granted, actually for the first time since the outbreak of hostilities in 1914.

Judges of the High Court were sent from Germany, and the trial was held in Cairo before what was virtually a world audience. The German legal lights wanted no slip-up in the bright glare under which they were performing, but they did not win the expected result. While the two German sailors admitted the burglary, they both denied killing Karam at the villa.

They had first gone to the villa on the night of January 13th, but sight of a man patrolling the grounds with a rifle had scared them away. They returned later on the following night, scaled the garden wall, breaking off one of the spikes with their weight, and bored a hole through the house door. At the trial no explanation was given as to how they came to know precisely where to drill or where to cut the bell wires.

They started a search of the ground floor and found some money in a vase. A chest in the same room was locked, and they could not force it open without making a great deal of noise. They climbed the stairs, Doelitzsch with a gun in his hand and Klauss gripping a jemmy. The gun had been stolen a short while before in Alexandria.

Here, on the upper floor, the two thieves parted company, or so they claimed. So did their stories about what actually happened. Doelitzsch maintained he went to the bedroom when Klauss was still in the dressing-room, but after exchanging weapons with him. He searched under the sleeping Karam's pillow, without explaining why. He was doing this, he said, when Klauss stupidly knocked over a vase and a chair, and the sound woke the sleeping Max Karam, who tried to jump out of bed and grapple with the man he saw through the mosquito curtain. In self-defence, so the German prisoner claimed, he struck the angry Karam over the head. Almost at the same moment as Karam reeled back Klauss ran into the room and from the right fired the gun he held at the man in the mosquito curtain.

The shot, Karam's falling, and the swift change of events all made Doelitzsch lose his nerve. He dropped the jemmy and ran out with Klauss. It wasn't until he was outside that he realised he was no longer holding the jemmy.

Doelitzsch said they had arrived back at their Alexandria lodging about half-past five.

However, when it was the turn of Klauss to relate how the killing occurred he told a very different story. He said they had not changed weapons and had, in fact, entered the sleeping man's room together, and Doelitzsch had told him to hit Karam over the head with the jemmy. But according to Klauss he hated violence and refused, whereupon the jemmy had been snatched from his hand and he retreated out of the room while Doelitzsch attacked the man in the bed. When he heard sounds of a scuffle he ran down the stairs, and it was when he reached the ground floor he heard the gunshot.

By this version Doelitzsch was saddled with both weapons.

It was fairly clear that each man was lying, trying to throw the actual murder on the other.

For a very good reason.

By German law at that time only the actual person committing a murder was guilty of it. A confederate who did not actually stay, even though he was present to commit another crime, was not guilty of murder by German law.

Unfortunately for Klauss the reconstruction of the crime as made by the Medico-Legal Department's experts was accepted by the court, which meant that both men struck the victim. The prosecution claimed Klauss had actually fired the shot, and argued that the medical evidence supported this as well as the other prisoner's first statement. The prosecution also claimed that Doelitzsch was an actual accomplice in murder by calling Klauss to help him when Karam showed fight.

The prosecution claimed premeditation because they had come armed and had stopped to fight with the awakened Karam instead of running away.

The defence did its best to show that premeditation was not a fact in this case. It could do little to show that neither man was actually not guilty.

Indeed, when all the pleas were on the record and all the

evidence had been given the only question remaining was the paramount one of who fired the shot? Because there could be no outright proof the court found both men guilty of the crime and sentenced each to penal servitude for life. By doing so a most important precedent had been created for other German judges presiding over a murder trial with two prisoners in the dock.

5

THE CASE OF THE MISSING LETTER

THE criminal dupe, who is human putty in the hands of a stronger, more dominant personality, has been a veritable serial character in sensational fiction throughout the twentieth century. If a real-life prototype were sought it might be found in Charles F. Jones, who was doing well enough until he met Albert T. Patrick a few weeks before the twentieth century dawned.

They met in an apartment in Madison Avenue, the current home of New York's slick young men in flannel suits who grow ulcers working for the world's most successful advertising agencies. So persuasive and forthright was Patrick he might have been the prototype, in his turn, for some of these later forceful characters with the convincing word and the cliché clincher.

A couple of years before, in 1897, Charles Jones had been tending a store in the Capitol Hotel in Houston, Texas. It was owned by William Rice, who was the active manager. He was also a widower without children, and was certainly lonely. He liked Jones and suggested the other leave the store and become his personal valet and secretary. Jones accepted, and became a personal friend of his employer's. When Rice moved to New York some time later it was natural for Jones to accompany him. They settled in a good-class apartment in Madison Avenue, where in November 1899 Albert T. Patrick appeared and saw Jones.

At the time William Rice was involved in an action concerning the estate of his late wife in Texas. Patrick, the slick New Yorker, told Jones that he was in search of testimony that would firmly establish Rice was no longer resident in Texas.

"You could help me, and it would be worth your while," he told Jones.

Jones more or less told the lawyer to go paddle his own canoe, in the idiom of the time, and he showed the visitor the door.

When Rice returned home Jones did not mention the caller or what the latter had wanted. He never explained this omission, but it is just possible that he had been having second thoughts about the possibility of making some quick easy money and escaping a life that was humdrum and showing little sign of becoming any different—except perhaps for the worst. For Rice was, by this time, virtually a recluse who had to be attended day and night.

However that may be, when some days later Patrick returned to try his luck again he was shown in, and when he talked Jones listened. Patrick was very persuasive. He took his time encouraging Jones's cupidity to grow roots and make some useful growth, and this required a number of visits to the Madison Avenue apartment, always in Rice's absence.

When Jones had the sweet smell of easy dollars under his nose he was induced to practise his master's signature, and when Patrick produced a letter requiring that signature Jones supplied it.

The forgery was an excellent job, for Jones had a sure eye and an artist's wrist movement.

The letter was an equally good job, for Patrick knew his law. By the terms of the forged letter William Rice withdrew from the pending litigation in Texas and gave as reason the fact that illegal residence in the State could be proved against him.

In their moments of exchanging confidences Patrick learned from his new dupe of a will Rice had made three years earlier. By its terms he left practically all of his three-million-dollar estate to a Houston college, the William Rice Institute, founded by Rice years before.

This news supplied the silver-tongued lawyer with a new theme, the unjustness of an old man who ignored the claims of those who had devoted their lives to him while he merely considered buying immortality in bricks and mortar. There was some old-fashioned blarney streaking Patrick's oratorical phrasing, and the mixture worked like yeast in Jones's mind. He came to see himself as the lawyer pictured him, a man forgotten and cheated by a man who should admit his obligations to another who had devoted himself and his life to the other's profit and comfort. It all sounded high-minded and somewhat high-flown, even, but Patrick knew precisely what he was doing by working on Jones's feelings and susceptibilities, and even his deep personal fears for the future.

It didn't take long before Jones was thinking of himself as a badly wronged man. True, this was little more than nonsense, but it was very dangerous nonsense, for to Jones had come what he considered enlightenment.

In this enlightened state he saw Patrick as the one man who considered what was best for Charles F. Jones.

He trusted Patrick, and because he trusted him he took his advice and did his bidding, which was all the conniving lawyer could ask. For Patrick had another forgery lined up. This time it was to yield a fantastic prize, the lawyer assured himself. The terms were outrageous, but Jones was by this time an acquiescent puppet of the man who was doing his thinking for him.

The master-mind produced the will. It was for the puppet to forge the testator's name to the bogus document.

The will produced by Patrick was one whereby Rice left the lawyer half his estate. There was no reason, apparently, why he should restrict his covetous greed. To make the signing all right by his tame forger the terms allowed a generous sum to be paid to Jones as a reward for past services. The residue was to go to Rice's natural heirs, presumably in the fond hope of stilling their anger at being cheated of what they had considered theirs in the first place. The canny lawyer insisted that Jones retype the will on a machine in the Madison Avenue apartment. After Patrick had read it through he told Jones to write in Rice's signature. It was after he had completed this work under Patrick's direction that Jones again indulged in second thoughts. This time his impulse was to destroy his fresh handiwork, but Patrick had the forged document, and, seeing how conscience possibly was working on Jones, the lawyer set himself to bolster the weakling's nerve and assure him that he had nothing to fear and everything to gain. Before he left the apartment Jones had certainly recovered his nerve.

The chief reason for the recovery was Patrick's assurance that the current genuine will did not have to be destroyed. In the first place, it would naturally be superseded by the later will, and in the second its production would serve to show the dead Rice's heirs how much they stood to gain under the terms of the second will as compared with the first, in which most of the estate went to the educational establishment in Houston.

"When they realise this fact," Patrick pointed out, "there will be much less chance of their deciding to contest it."

However, having bolstered Jones's drooping morale, Patrick discovered, without realising it, that he had oversold himself on the cleverness of the forged will, and he began to consider the possibility of bettering its terms for himself.

It was over a period of months that he came gradually to the decision that he could well take the risk of contriving yet a third will. He went to see Jones on a hot June day and told him they had now better make out a fresh will. He produced the document he wanted Jones to copy out and sign.

Jones read it through and immediately registered a vigorous protest.

"I'm not mentioned in it, and you're the sole executor."

Patrick smiled at the other's show of indignation. "You must trust me," he insisted gently. "This way I can take even better care of you when I myself have full control over the estate. Don't you see?"

Jones was finding it very difficult to see anything at all at the moment. Patrick proceeded to con him again, cleverly and unscrupulously, and after a fresh show of a resistance that was visibly weakening Jones gave way and typed out the new will and forged his employer's signature at the end.

The signatures of two witnesses were appended. One was named Potts, the other David Short. They were hirelings for a price whom Patrick could produce at short notice.

In possession of this third will, Patrick decided the smart thing to do would be to establish friendship between himself and the man who was due to leave him control of his estate. To avoid trouble and suspicion that friendship had to be observed and noted. While he could not rely upon Rice taking to him as a person, he could certainly be sure that visual evidence would be available later when required.

To this end he cajoled Jones into writing him about thirty warm letters couched in the friendliest of terms, and all appreciative in tone of the services Patrick was rendering the writer. The signature at the close of each letter, of course, was William Rice's as forged by Jones.

In one of the letters there was a cautious reference to a new will and a mention of changed beneficiaries. In a second there was a peeved reference to the William Rice Institute, for which the writer claimed to have done enough in his lifetime, and to his family heirs, whom the writer considered to have secured sufficient from him.

Each letter had a carbon copy taken, and all were dated at carefully calculated intervals to cover a fair period of time. The carbon copies were inserted in the file of his master's outgoing correspondence that was kept in order by Jones.

It was a cleverly contrived lie that would take a good deal of detecting for what it actually was.

But Patrick couldn't rest from working at his great scheme to secure the Rice fortune for himself. His restive legal brains were constantly contriving new ways of reinforcing his claims and of securing his interests firmly. It wasn't long before he met Jones again and produced yet another document for the valet and secretary to copy. Its terms instructed Patrick to go ahead without further delay and take over the control of securities worth in total some millions of dollars. Such an instruction, to Patrick's devious mind, provided the keystone in the arch of confidence he had architected.

As previously Jones performed as ordered. The time had passed when he had second thoughts. He could no longer face such reconsideration of his false position. He had become utterly dependent on the man who had turned him into a crook.

Patrick became anxious to handle some money transactions before the turn of natural events gave him the opportunity he had arranged. He told Jones to hold back three cheques signed by Rice himself. In their stead the persons to whom the cheques were drawn as payment received substitute cheques with Jones's forgery in place of the genuine Rice signature. Patrick in this way secured a trial run, as it were, of the forged signature. If a cheque were queried by Rice's bank the old man, who was now eighty-four, would insist that the signature was his because he knew he had signed the cheque. Such a challenge and such a refutation could be insurance for the future.

However, none of the dud cheques was queried. All three were accepted and the amounts credited to the payee without any come-back from Rice's bank.

Patrick felt he had good reason for congratulating himself on picking Jones to do his crooked work. Not only that, but Jones was now an established criminal. His forgeries had been used. Jones was utterly committed past any chance of withdrawing from the net in which he had become ensnared.

The lawyer's attention was next turned to the old man who cooked his own cereal foods and suffered acute indigestion as a result.

He had another conference with Jones, who was curiously silent and not able to make any protest at Patrick's proposed scheme, behaviour of which the lawyer approved. Charles F. Jones had, in truth, become his creature.

When the next bout of acid indigestion made life barely tolerable for the aged millionaire Jones played his allotted part and counselled calling a physician. The doctor who arrived was one sent by Patrick. He prescribed some pills, but these were removed from their bottle and pills of a mercury compound substituted. Rice supplied them to Jones.

Mercury agreed even less with William Rice's worn-out stomach than the acid he had been making in his intestines. He became really ill, and the nimble-witted Patrick had Jones prepare a fresh letter. This was to the effect that, in the event of his death, William Rice required his body to be cremated.

It was just a precaution on the part of the man who was prepared to bend the law into a hoop he could bowl along like a child's toy. Mercury would leave traces in the body. Those traces could never be found if that body was cremated.

When he was reasonably certain that the patient was failing past recovery Patrick dictated a letter Jones was to send to his brother in Texas, who was a chemist. Jones asked for some chloroform to be dispatched to him. If the brother wondered at being asked to send chloroform several thousand miles to a city like New York, where it must be in good supply, he made no query or protest.

The chloroform arrived at the address in Madison Avenue.

From that moment the death of William Rice was no longer in doubt. It had been arranged for and was to be accelerated. William Rice, the rich old recluse who had been living in a world of cruel make-believe for the past months, was about to be murdered.

And of course the dupe Jones was to be the willing tool of the brain that planned the crime.

For Patrick was now losing some of his natural caution, in his haste to get his hands on the Rice fortune, and his overweening confidence was about to bring stark tragedy to several lives.

Ten months had passed since Patrick had first met Charles Jones at the Madison Avenue apartment. In that time both men had come a long way in villainy and in their strange interdependence on each other, one from weakness, the other from what he considered as strength.

Both were awaiting an expected event.

It was on the 16th of September that a wire was sent to the very ill millionaire from Texas. It contained the advice that one of his oil plants had been gutted by fire. Funds were required to start immediate repairs. Rice decided to transfer money from his New York bank. He dictated a telegram to Jones, but the man who had sold his loyalty for a promise from another man did not send the wire. He realised that Rice could not last much longer and to have the money transferred from New York to Texas would empty Rice's account of most of its current funds.

The dire news from Texas in some perverse manner roused the fighting spirit of the old man. He took a turn for the better. It was as though he was willing himself to be well and active again, and able to tackle problems as they arose.

The following morning he demanded a normal breakfast and ate with obvious enjoyment after having had a good night's sleep. Jones was alarmed at this about-face in the old man's condition, and notified Patrick, who lost his easy confidence and came to a decision he had been putting off in the hope that he had already done enough to ensure that William Rice died in his bed with a minimum of trouble for everyone.

But the old man was obstinate.

So was Patrick.

"You'll have to chloroform him," he told Jones. "You've got the stuff, and although I'd hoped it wouldn't come to this, now there's no alternative. He can't live to find out you didn't send that wire to Texas."

"No, I'm not doing it."

Jones got the words out from between his teeth, but he made them sound more like a protest than a conviction he would stand by. Patrick looked at him, smiled thinly, and began the old arguments all over again.

In the end, with the same result. Jones could wriggle, but he couldn't escape. He was trapped. Recovery of the man lying in bed and thinking of when he could leave it would spell disaster for the false secretary. Jones would not be able to avoid being uncovered for what he was, and he would then face certain imprisonment.

He agreed to do as Patrick suggested.

"Wait till I've gone," said the lawyer who always considered his own interests first, "and do it when he's asleep."

Before he left he gave his dupe careful instructions about how to pour some of the liquid chloroform into a sponge, wrap the lethal sponge in a twisted towel and place the towel over the sleeping man's face, so that his lungs filled with the drugging vapour.

Within a few hours Jones had carried out these instructions, but having done them he lost his nerve and ran from the room, leaving the towel over the pale whiskery face. He knew he had to recover his nerve before he could go back into the room. Before this happened he was shocked by the ringing of the front-door bell. Peering from a window, he saw two elderly ladies who were friends of the man he had tried to kill. They bore a gift of home-made cakes and wine. When no one replied to their ringing they went away, and Jones returned to the old man's bedroom to find he was dead.

It was a Sunday. The date was September 23rd, 1900.

Charles Jones could not tell himself the better the day, the better the deed. As a matter of fact, he could not tell himself anything that would be comforting. He was a murderer and that was a status nothing could change.

He was also a man who had run completely out of the kind of short-term luck he had been enjoying, if that term applies in his case. For the old ladies outside the apartment had heard him scampering from the murder room, and had wondered much when their ringing was not answered.

When they left Madison Avenue they discussed a situation that seemed somehow very wrong, and decided they should go to the police. They called at a police station and explained about their visit to a sick friend, and how their ringing the doorbell had not been answered by the valet they had heard inside the apartment.

The facts were jotted down, and the old ladies left the police station. The police, however, did nothing. It wasn't the first time they had been visited by old ladies whose fears had involved them in awkward inquiries because those fears had proved groundless.

The following day, Monday the 24th of September, David Short, who had been a witness to William Rice's forged will, walked into the Swenson Bank and pushed across the polished counter a cheque for twenty-three thousand dollars. It was made payable to Abert T. Patrick and was signed by one of the bank's substantial clients, William T. Rice. The teller who handled the cheque had smart eyes and the kind of pernickety mind that belongs behind a bank counter. He saw that the slip of paper had been endorsed by Albert T. Patrick, which was a difference of one vital letter.

He pushed the cheque back at Short.

"This cheque is incorrectly endorsed," he said. "It must be correctly endorsed before I can pay out on it."

"Why, what do you mean?" said the puzzled and slightly alarmed Short.

"Look for yourself, sir," said the teller. "It is made out to

Abert, but has been endorsed by Albert. I cannot accept that difference."

Short snatched up the cheque and hurried from the bank. He was back a short time later with the cheque endorsed this time by Abert T. Patrick. When he re-presented it he was told payment could not be made, as it had been learned that William Rice had recently died. Again Short picked up the colourful piece of paper that the Swenson Bank was reluctant to accept, and left in a rather nervous fashion.

What had happened between his visits was that the bank's employee had phoned the Madison Avenue apartment and spoken to Jones about the cheque, who had told him it was quite in order without bothering to consult Mr. Rice. The teller had gone to Eric Swenson and explained the unusual situation.

"Get in touch with Mr. Rice," he was told. "We can only make payment if we have his personal assurance he wants us to cash it."

The man had thereupon rung the Madison Avenue apartment again, and said he had to speak to Mr. Rice in person to be able to clear the cheque. That was putting Jones in an impossible position, which he promptly demonstrated by admitting that his employer had died the previous evening.

The teller informed Eric Swenson, who had no hesitation in ordering, "Stop payment on the cheque."

So that when Patrick himself came back with the cheque the teller was prepared to tell him why payment was being withheld. Whereupon Patrick became insistent that the dead man's cheque should be honoured.

"It could take a long time before his estate is cleared," he pointed out in a restrained fury at being balked by what he considered a rather deep shade of red tape.

He was passed on to Eric Swenson, who didn't like his visitor's looks and was affronted by his manner. The banker's own manner remained decidedly cool and certainly uncompromising.

"We can't cash that cheque now, Mr. Patrick," he maintained. "I'm sorry, but that's how it is."

Patrick left with the worthless piece of paper, but he was not leaving behind him a state of things as they had been, for the banker rang up his legal adviser and explained what had happened, and in turn he was advised to get in touch with the District Attorney.

He had no reluctance in doing this, for he wanted to keep his bank clear of any dubious transaction that could result in adverse publicity. He found the District Attorney very ready to listen, and also to have his office act with more promptness than the precinct police visited by the two elderly ladies only hours before.

The D.A.'s office discovered, upon making inquiry, that three cheques totalling not far short of a quarter of a million dollars and made payable by Rice to Patrick had been cleared by the former's account at the Fifth Avenue Trust Company. Moreover, a man named Potts had cleared a fourth cheque, for twenty-five thousand dollars, which had been paid into Patrick's account.

Potts, it transpired, shared an office with Albert Patrick.

The D.A.'s investigators recovered the four cheques and upon examination it was found that the payer's signature was identical on each. It was as though a traced signature had been used. This similarity pointed to forgery in the eyes of the men who knew how forgers worked.

The D.A.'s office contacted the police. The elderly ladies' complaint was taken from a dead file, and, somewhat late but all the more determined for that reason, detectives visited the Rice apartment at 500 Madison Avenue, which was in mourning. The detectives were shown into the apartment by a nervous Charles Jones, who explained that he had been Mr. Rice's valet and personal secretary. Seated in an armchair in the comfortable living-room was Albert Patrick, nattily dressed, with a trimmed beard, which he stroked gently. He introduced himself as the late William Rice's attorney.

He confessed himself puzzled as to why a visit from the police had been deemed necessary. Mr. Rice had died quietly in his sleep, with his valet in attendance, and a death certificate had been signed by the physician who had attended him during his recent illness.

Patrick was very smooth and seemingly in no way upset by the death of a valued client. The detectives stalled about the reason for their visit while a police surgeon hurried to join them. After he had viewed the body he ordered it to be taken to the local morgue. This was the moment when Patrick produced the letter prepared for such a contingency.

"Mr. Rice always wished to have his body cremated," he explained.

But he was out-smarted. The body was removed over his wishes and the letter he had flourished was not returned to him. The signature on it was found to be another of the too-similar forgeries.

The police autopsy proved the cause of death given on the death certificate to be inaccurate. There it was stated to be senile weakness of the heart. William Rice's heart may have been weak, but tests proved he had died from chloroform poisoning, which was murder.

By the time murder was proved Jones had been arrested on a charge of forgery and taken from Madison Avenue. Patrick was arrested on a similar charge while he was at Rice's safe-deposit company, arguing with officials as to why they should release in his custody, as the dead William Rice's attorney, some valuable securities Rice had locked in thair vaults. Keeping him company, perhaps as a witness, was the shadowy figure of his office mate, Potts. Patrick turned to him after being told he was under arrest and said, "Telephone my attorney." Then he turned back to the detectives and asked, "Has Jones been arrested?"

Jones was actually in a state of collapse, as Patrick very soon discovered for himself, for he was placed in the next cell to his dupe.

Within a few hours a Mr. Baker from Houston arrived in New York. He was a close relative of the dead man, and carried in his pocket a telegram he had received from Jones. It ran:

"Mr. Rice died 8 o'clock last night under care physician. Death certificate 'old age weak heart delirium.' Left instructions to be interred in Milwaukee with remains of wife. Funeral 10 a.m. tomorrow at 500 Madison Avenue. Jones."

The wire had been dispatched on the Monday when David Short made his futile visits to the Swenson Bank.

The relative from Texas showed the police a copy of the reply he had wired to New York:

"Please make no disposition of Rice's remains until we arrive. We leave tonight. Arrive New York Thursday morning."

This telegram notwithstanding, Patrick had already gone ahead with giving instructions for the body to be cremated, but the police intervention had frustrated this.

Patrick, however, was not finished with violence—or with his dupe. He wanted Jones removed, and almost succeeded in a fresh piece of villainy. It was after Jones was brought back to his cell from questioning in the D.A.'s office that Patrick handed him, from the next cell, his pocket-knife, choosing a moment when the guard was absent, and saying in a heavy stage whisper that was like a command, "Here, use this. The jig's up and we're done for. You go first and I'll follow."

In a state bordering on petrified terror Jones took the knife, opened the larger of the two blades and slashed at his throat.

But he was a poor hand at committing suicide.

When the guard returned Jones was found lying on the floor of his cell in a pool of blood. He was groaning, but a far cry from being a corpse, although he was in no shape to talk, which was what the D.A. wanted. He was patched up in hospital, and while mending was induced to turn State's Evidence against the man who had directed his life from that day in the previous November when they first met. This meant that Patrick was brought to trial for the murder without Jones being charged, for the latter was now the State's chief witness, and his testimony would convict the prisoner.

When he appeared at his trial Patrick did not attempt the impossible by refuting Jones's story. Instead, he tried to shake a solid attack on him by arguing that there was no established proof of murder. The experts had agreed that the dead man's lungs had become congested with chloroform, but he submitted this had been caused by embalming fluid. Such a claim bore the true stamp of Patrick's wily thinking. But to give a little more weight to the defence he insisted that if murder had been committed, if the chloroform had been responsible for the congestion of the dead man's lungs, the person responsible for this was Jones.

Nevertheless, he was found guilty by the jury that listened to the evidence, and Albert T. Patrick was duly sentenced to death.

However, there was a good deal of grudging sympathy with a man in his position, a rogue who had been sentenced for a crime he had set up but not committed, while the criminal who had performed the murder was released in return for his testimony on behalf of the State of New York.

In deference to public opinion, more than for any other reason, Patrick was saved from death by having his sentence commuted to life imprisonment.

However, he did not die a convict. When the uproar created by the Rice murder and the trial of one of the criminals had been forgotten, like Patrick himself, he was pardoned and released from Sing Sing, to disappear in obscurity, as Charles Jones had succeeded in doing years before.

6

THE CASE OF THE LONELY DESERTER

SUMMER tourists on their way to the Scottish Highlands who look for a suitable postcard to send to friends are frequently puzzled by a view of a small hut near some trees at the far side of a not very interesting expanse of moorland which is still for sale among more modern pictorial cards.

The legend beneath the rather dreary card is "Toplis's Hut."

Who, they want to know not unnaturally, was Toplis?

Nearly fifty years ago he was the most hunted man in Britain, and the hunt for Percy Toplis was in its time the greatest manhunt undertaken by police in Wales, England, and Scotland. Toplis was a killer. He was a challenge to every policeman in the British Isles because they were all his enemies. He shot at several. He died under fire from a police posse.

He was a renegade, a deserter, and a vicious thief.

He first made the national headlines in 1920.

It was a bright spring day in that year when a farm labourer in Hampshire came upon the body of a dead man. There was blood on the corpse, and its hands were folded into fists and outflung as though at the moment of death the man had been protesting or trying to ward off an assailant. The farm labourer, whose name was Burridge, peered close at his grisly find and realised that he was observing the results of murder, for the cause of the blood that had run down the man's coat and congealed was an ugly wound that had destroyed the back of the victim's head.

He straightened and hurried on to the farm at Thruxton Down where he worked. He told the farmer of the man he had first thought was a tramp lying asleep under a hedge. The farmer got in touch with the constable in the nearby village, who phoned the police station in Andover. Before long detectives were searching the dead man's pockets.

In one they came upon a driving licence made out in the name of George Spicer, who had an address in Salisbury. Another pocket held a clasp-knife and some personal papers. They found no money.

The killing appeared to have an obvious motive—robbery. Also, lines made in the soft turf leading to where the body was found suggested that it had been dragged some distance from the road.

When the Salisbury police were contacted it was quickly learned that George Spicer was not unknown to them. He was a taxi driver in the city. He had no police record, and was a man generally liked, who worked long hours, and was invariably civil and helpful to his passengers.

A man believed to have no enemies who would shoot him in the back of the head and then rifle his pockets of loose change and currency to make his death appear the result of greed. George Spicer, in fact, was known to live an uncomplicated life, driving a Darracq touring model with mica curtains. He was a man familiar to many of the soldiers who came into the city from their camp on Salisbury Plain.

He was known to be obliging to men in uniform who had missed the last bus and were anxious to get back to camp. Because he was obliging he found them generous with tips. He was believed to make good money with his taxi. The chances were that on any normal working day he would carry a useful sum in banknotes in his pocket.

The Hampshire police had no doubts as to why George Spicer was found with no cash in his pockets but with a hole in his head and cast away in a lonely part of the county.

Someone had hired his cab and told him to drive to where he could be conveniently slaughtered. It had happened to other taxi drivers. It would happen to many more. Death in a deserted backwater area was an occupational hazard for hire-car drivers of any kind.

The post mortem established that Spicer had been shot in the back of the head at reasonably close quarters with a firearm that was most likely a Service revolver. There were dark powder burns on some of the short hairs in the nape of the neck and on the flesh. It was considered possible that the killer had shot the taxi driver from the back seat.

The day when Mrs. Spicer was told she was a widow and her two children orphans was April 25. Her dead husband's twelve-horsepower car was missing. What she wasn't told, in order to spare her feelings at the time, was that the bullet that entered George Spicer's head and abruptly ended his twenty-seven years of life was of the cruel dum-dum type, declared illegal by the Geneva Convention. Its pointed nose had been tampered with, so that upon impact the metal spread out. The surgeon who undertook the post mortem found it flattened against the frontal bone of the dead taxi driver's skull.

George Spicer had been alive one instant, dead the next, in less time than it takes a clock to tick.

The post mortem reported scratch marks on the victim's face. These were grooved into the forehead and face. There were small particles of gravel half buried in the flesh covering the cheeks, nose, and forehead. The gravel chips were identified as tiny scraps of road metal. The police considered their implication and decided that perhaps Spicer had been told to drive to some out-of-the-way place, and had got out of his seat to feel for change in a pocket.

While he was preoccupied in this way he had been shot down

and his body then dragged by the ankles off the road or lane, to be left under the bush where Burridge had found it.

The killer had picked up any money that had dropped, removed such cash as he found in the dead man's pockets, and then driven away in the Darracq.

The manhunt that was started for the unknown killer began at the cab-rank where George Spicer usually waited, with a foot on the running board and a smouldering cigarette between his lips.

It didn't take the detectives on the case long to trace a couple of Servicemen who had been in the company of two women when they asked Spicer to drive them out to the camp, where large numbers of men who had been trained for a war that had ended on November 11th, 1918, were waiting to be demobbed officially.

Other drivers who used Spicer's favourite rank told the plain-clothes men that on the day he was murdered the dead man had complained of trade being slack. It was late when he was asked to drive out to the camp by the two soldiers and their female companions, but he had agreed and had set out from the city along the Andover road.

When he was only a short distance from Andover he had found his petrol was low and had pulled in at a garage that was open late. After the tank had been filled, and when he was about to climb back into the driving seat, a silent-footed figure had walked up out of the night.

"How about a lift as far as Amesbury?" the newcomer had inquired.

He had then turned and seen the car had passengers, and muttered, "Hell, just my luck!"

George Spicer, for whom trade had been slack, saw a chance to make a few shillings on the return journey.

"I can't take you now," he told the stranger in the soft darkness beyond the lights of the garage. "However, if you wait till I'm back from Bulford I'll take you then."

The four inside the Darracq heard the stranger say, "All right, that'll do me. I'll wait."

He was still standing there in the shadows as the Darracq's headlamps washed over the road and Spicer turned to head for Bulford.

The two soldiers and their companions were asked to provide the police with a description of this stranger. None of them could offer one that would have been helpful to identify the man, though one of them had been left with the idea that the stranger had been an officer, and another said he had spoken with what could have been a North Country accent. He had remained where his cap badge and face were not seen distinctly.

The Hampshire police sent the following request to all police stations throughout England and Wales:

"Watch for Darracq 12 h.p. open tourer, painted grey, upholstered black leather, with Riley wire wheels, registration number AM 2290. May be driven by soldier wearing British warm. Soldier is armed and likely to shoot if approached."

The British warm referred to was the familiar greatcoat of the British Tommy in World War I.

Newspaper readers in Britain picked up their morning paper on April 26th to learn that a vast manhunt was being mounted throughout the country for a killer in uniform. By that time police were making routine checks at garages and petrol stations and lookouts were being posted at busy traffic junctions throughout a wide area around Salisbury.

Separate inquiries were started at Bulford Camp, where detectives took down scores of statements from Servicemen and collected a list of known deserters. They ran down a number of promising leads, but found nothing helpful in the murder hunt for George Spicer's killer.

However, a private soldier named Holdrick, who had been away in Southampton on the 24th, offered some information that sounded at least hopeful.

He said he had been stopped by a man he knew to be a deserter. This man had been on the run from the M.P.s since the beginning of the year. He was lonely and fed up, and when he saw Holdrick's familiar face he instinctively called to him.

Holdrick had shown his surprise.

"What happened to you?" he asked the deserter.

"I took one of the camp cars on Boxing Night. After that I wasn't going back," the man grinned.

"What did you do with it?" Holdrick inquired.

"Flogged it in Gloucester for four hundred quid. What I did then I can do again, even if I've got to try some persuasion."

He had then pulled a Webley revolver from his overcoat pocket and twisted it with a quick wrist action under Holdrick's nose.

"You must be mad," Holdrick had told him.

At that the deserter had laughed, pocketed his bulky revolver, and drawn his overcoat closer over the sergeant-major's uniform he was wearing. The last Holdrick saw of the man was walking down a Southampton street.

"What was this deserter's name?" Holdrick was asked by the police.

"Percy Toplis," was the answer.

There was no immediate way of finding out what had become of the deserter named Toplis who had been armed on the 24th with a weapon of a kind that had fired the shot that killed George Spicer. But they learned that a private named Fallows had been friendly with Toplis. When they made inquiries as to Fallows' whereabouts they were told he had vanished from the camp only a short while ago.

In fact, on the night Spicer was murdered.

But the inquiring detectives also found someone who was able to tell them that, a short time before Fallows disappeared, a man dressed in a sergeant-major's uniform came into the cook-house where Fallows was on duty and had asked for a cup of tea, which had been served to him.

Fallows couldn't be traced, but in their hunt for this man the police learned more about Toplis. For instance, they came by the information that the man with the Webley had been going about the countryside dodging the M.P.s and calling himself Sergeant-Major Wilson. He had been wearing the ribbons of several campaigns and also those of the D.C.M. and M.M.

But even the dubious Sergeant-Major Wilson had apparently vanished by the time the police heard of him.

The first real lead came from as far away as Swansea, in South Wales.

A constable on his beat in the Welsh town observed a parked grey touring car, its hood down and with mica side-curtains. Seated in the front were two soldiers. He glanced at the one behind the wheel. He was wearing the familiar British warm of the war years and under the peak of an officer's cap were a pair of gold-rimmed glasses. The observant constable took in the car's make. A Darracq.

Also its number. AM 2290.

Unfortunately the constable's excitement at his discovery did not make for a necessary caution. He started across the pavement calling to the driver, "Hey, just a minute." The driver had no minutes to give him. The engine suddenly roared, and the grey car was off down the street and spinning around a corner in a tight turn with wheels screeching a rubbery protest. Although the unfortunate constable had lost it almost before he had found it, the grey car was discovered again, not very far away. It had been abandoned in a back-street.

The murder car had been recovered.

The news gave heart to the detectives organising the dragnet that was intended to snare a wanted killer. Front pages of newspapers claimed that it would not be long before Toplis was found and arrested. There were great and widespread hopes that George Spicer's callous killer would shortly be where he could no longer be a menace.

Such hopes were to be slowly dissipated as time went by with no arrest and no news likely to lead to one.

In Swansea the Welsh police searched every street and questioned scores of persons. Such a lengthy investigation got nowhere. The grey tourer's two soldiers had been swallowed up in the surrounding countryside. The only positive outcome of the time and effort expended was the reasonable certainty that the man seen behind the wheel of the grey car was Percy Toplis.

After a fruitless two days of unrelenting inquiry and checking, something quite unexpected occurred.

Private Fallows arrived back at Bulford, where he was sighted by a watchful M.P. and arrested for desertion. The civil police were informed, and a car arrived with detectives who requested the military to hand over Fallows. They claimed they wanted him as an accessary after the fact of murder.

"What's all this about?" demanded a seemingly mystified soldier who was regretting having had second thoughts about going back to camp.

He was informed in considerable detail when he appeared before the local Hampshire magistrates. At that he again appeared at a loss.

"The first I heard about the taxi murder was when I got back to Bulford," he protested.

The magistrates heard him out. According to the deserter's story, Toplis had come up to him on the night of the murder while he was working in the cook-house. The man in a sergeant-major's uniform, who had been AWOL since the previous January, had told Fallows that he had got a car.

"I'm taking it to South Wales," Toplis confided. "I know a man down there who'll take it off my hands. You want to come along?"

The man telling the story to the listening magistrates explained that he had always got along with Toplis. Moreover, Toplis had admitted he would prefer to make the run with some company.

Fallows, at the time, was feeling fed to the back teeth with camp life and Army routine, and was longing for the time when he could become a civilian again. The demobbing process seemed to be taking too long, although he was not unique in feeling this. Fallows felt that any change would be one for the better.

He had told Toplis, "All right, I'll come for the ride, Perce. But I've got to get back when you've sold it."

Toplis had grinned back at him and promised easily, "When I've collected for the car you can have your fare back. Just thought you'd like the change."

Any fears about the prospect had been resolved, for Fallows, by this promise. Or so he claimed. But he admitted his fear had returned in a hurry when he took his seat beside Toplis in the grey tourer parked outside the camp. As he sat down he saw the Webley revolver, lying where Toplis had left it.

"Why do you want this?" he asked, pointing to the weapon.

Toplis had finished lighting a cigarette before saying nonchalantly, "Oh, just in case."

Before Fallows could get out of the car Toplis had started up the engine and was driving off. Fallows had been unable to bring himself to ask the other to stop and let him out. He felt committed to the ride. Besides, Percy Toplis could be a man who might take such a request the wrong way. Especially after his passenger had seen the Webley.

Fallows had said no more about it, but had settled down for the long night ride.

Toplis had driven as far as Savernake Forest, where he drew up under a cluster of large trees.

"This'll do," he said as he switched off the car's lights.

"Do for what?" Fallows had asked.

Toplis made no reply. Instead, he reached for a bundle of clothing rolled up on the car's back seat and for a can of petrol. He walked away under the trees, drenched the bundle of clothes with petrol, and set it alight. He waited some distance away, watching until the bundle had been consumed and the petrol flames had died down. Then he came back to the car, climbed in and switched on the lights, and started up the engine again.

"What was all that about?" Fallows asked.

For the second time he received no reply to a question. He had decided it would be wise to let the matter drop. Toplis had his reasons. Let it go at that.

They had reached Swansea the morning of the next day, the 25th, which was a Sunday, and the city wore a deserted look with shops shut and streets empty. They drove to a modest hotel and Toplis booked a room for them.

"I'm going to stretch out," he had announced, and went to bed, taking the revolver with him. "I feel safer with it," he had added when he saw Fallows looking at him oddly.

On the Monday he left the hotel and returned in a bad mood, for he had failed to sell the car to the man he had expected to take it off his hands.

He told Fallows angrily, "The damned fool thinks I've pinched it."

Toplis began to act nervously. He paid the bill at that hotel and the pair of uneasy friends went to another. After booking the new room Toplis went for a drive round Swansea, and suddenly roused the interest of an observant constable who risked his life without knowing it by running across the pavement and shouting at the man behind the wheel. Toplis had raced off and a few minutes later let Fallows out.

"I know where I can get rid of it. See you at the hotel," he had shouted before driving off.

Later he told his now very anxious companion that he had let someone have the car without enlarging on the deal. The pair had made for the station, where Toplis had bought two single tickets, one to London, the other to Salisbury. Fallows had seen him for the last time on a platform at Cardiff, where he had to change trains. He had made his way straight back to

Bulford, and inside the camp he had heard for the first time of the taxi murder and the hunt for Toplis.

"I haven't seen a paper," he said, "since I went off with Perce in the grey car."

His story was considered carefully by the Hampshire magistrates, who decided it sounded sufficiently convincing and discharged the prisoner. Private Fallows had ample reason for believing he had been very lucky.

His story served to intensify the endeavours being made to find the deserter with the Webley revolver. It was reported in the newspapers, and one result would be certain. Percy Toplis would not go out of his way to choose a companion again. He was now on his own, committed to the loneliness of the hunted deserter who is known to be a desperate and violent character.

Fallows had said Toplis had bought a ticket to London. That news switched the main search to the Metropolis. In the meantime reports about Toplis being seen and his predatory excursions poured into police stations all over the country. He was said to have held up motorists, burgled houses and private premises, and rifled the tills in shops.

Toplis, too, was having his run of luck. After leaving the Welsh express at Paddington he had crossed London to the Union Jack Club for Servicemen in the Waterloo Road, where he turned in early and had a good night's sleep. The next day he took a bus to the East End, where he walked into a barber's and had his dark moustache shaved off. But he didn't like the look of the strange face he saw staring back at him from the barber's mirror.

"Know where I can buy a moustache like the one you've just removed?" he asked the surprised barber, who said he didn't.

Toplis left the shop and continued east to Tilbury, where he made inquiries and learned that painters were required to work aboard a ship leaving for Dundee. Toplis applied for one of the jobs, was taken on, and worked his passage to Scotland wielding a paint brush.

As soon as he stepped on to Scottish soil he bought a newspaper and on the front page stared at himself with his familiar moustache. He made for a working-class restaurant, where he had a meal, read the account of the hunt to find him, and then he took from his pocket a small diary, which he liked to keep up to date. Under the heading April 30 he wrote: "Photographs. Worse luck Dundee."

Unfortunately he did not feel the curt memo required enlarging upon.

He did not stay in the town, but journeyed to Aberdeen, where someone reported having seen him to the police. However, when a close search was made he had vanished. His little well-thumbed diary established that on the day he was reported in Aberdeen he was actually in that grey city.

While more reports of his being seen in various well-spaced places reached the police, who had the task of checking all such information, Toplis was tramping into the Highlands. He reached Tomintoul, which has been described as the highest village in the British Isles. He told several farmers in the district that he was James Williamson. They employed him to do odd jobs and he earned enough to buy food. He slept in the small hut that was later photographed and made the subject of a picture postcard, numbers of which are still on sale, for the Highland Scots throw little away that they have paid money for, and presumably pictures of "Toplis's Hut" are still being bought by tourists to the Highlands. A few years back a relation of mine sent me one as a curiosity.

Toplis was an intruder in the hut, which had been built originally for the use of gamekeepers. When he lit a fire and smoke was seen coming from the hut's chimney a native of Tomintoul named James Grant reported the fact to the local constable. In company with a gamekeeper named Mackenzie, Constable Greig and his informant tramped off to investigate.

They entered the hut and found a man lying on a pile of bracken. He was alseep and by his head lay a grubby haversack. The constable bent down and shook the sleeper's shoulder. Toplis awoke and grabbed the Webley from the haversack when he saw Constable Greig's uniform.

He fired three shots. The constable fell to the floor, dying, a bullet in his lung. Grant collapsed with his spine smashed. Only Mackenzie escaped by bounding through the open door and running behind the hut and down the glen. Toplis sprang after him, stopped to jump on Greig's cycle, and went pedalling past the scared gamekeeper, who bounded away from him. The sight made Toplis laugh. Instead of shooting at the Highlander, he waved to him and called, "Cheerio!" in a tone of goodbye.

The cycle was left later in Glenkindle and Toplis set out on foot for Alford. When the police reached that place and found their quarry's scent cold they decided he had headed north.

Actually he was gyrating towards all points of a Scottish compass, south, west, north, and again south. The truth was he had lost his hunters, and reports came from Wales of his being seen there. He must have read of this report in a newspaper, for in his grubby diary he made an entry under May 24th: "The hunt on in West Wales. Some hopes."

A little less than a fortnight later he was in Edinburgh, for in that city he pawned his wristwatch on June 4th. His diary entry for the same day was a laconic: "Poor old wristwatch." He kept the pawn ticket. Presumably as a memento, for he had small chance of redeeming his pledged watch.

He headed south-west across country for Carlisle, the weather dry and warm, so that he could sleep out at night.

Two days after Toplis had pawned his watch Constable Fulton of the Cumberland Constabulary was walking home to High Hesket and the tea his wife would have waiting for him. He came upon an airman lying with his hands cupped under his head and his knees drawn up. The man was resting. With a three-day growth of beard he looked more like a tramp than a

Serviceman entitled to wear R.A.F. blue. When the airman saw Fulton he jumped to his feet and stood grinning at the constable. It took some moments for the truth to hit the Cumberland policeman, but when it did he was smart enough not to panic. He knew it was Toplis and that the killer had shot down two men not many days before at Tomintoul, one a Scots constable. P.C. Fulton must have realised the grinning man was as likely to kill him as not if the irrational notion took him to commit murder again.

He acted as though he had not recognised the most wanted man in Britain. Nodding to Toplis he asked where he was making for, a normal question in such circumstances.

"Penrith," Toplis said without hesitation. "I've overstayed my leave."

"It'll be a waste of time making for Penrith," Constable Fulton said, keeping to his role of an inquiring helper of strangers in the district. He gave the grinning desperado direction for reaching the nearest R.A.F. depot. "That'll save you time," he said, and then risked playing it very natural indeed. "You could be that chap Toplis," he added, with a laugh. "He's smart, keeping out of everyone's way."

Toplis remained grinning, enjoying the joke as he said, "Well, that let's me out. I'm not smart."

He turned around and walked down the road in the direction suggested by Constable Fulton, who continued on his way home, where he re-read through an official description of Toplis in a wanted handout. There was nothing about being in R.A.F. uniform in the latest description of Percy Toplis, but Constable Fulton was convinced by what he had read that he had recently spoken to Toplis. He said nothing to his wife about his intention, but got out his cycle and set out after the bearded airman. He continued until he knew he must have passed him. Then he stopped and propped the cycle against a tree. He heard movement and stepped into the wood beyond the lane, to find himself confronted by Toplis with his gun levelled.

"Drop your truncheon and handcuffs," the killer ordered, "and get out or I'll kill you like the others."

Toplis's mood had changed. The grin had gone. Fulton had no alternative. He went back to his cycle and rode home. He phoned Penrith, changed into an ordinary suit, and then started the eleven-mile journey to his local headquarters. He reached Penrith police station while arrangements were being made for a cordon to be thrown round the wood where Toplis had last been seen. The police were handed revolvers. They climbed into a car, and Fulton returned with them.

After some miles Fulton saw a man walking ahead.

"That's Toplis," he said.

The man was not in R.A.F. uniform and was carrying a brown-paper parcel. When he heard the car he looked round hopefully, then saw the police uniforms and jumped back. The brown-paper parcel changed hands and Toplis drew out the Webley. By this time the car had stopped and police were out and running swiftly towards him. He fired two hurried shots, both of which missed, and then the police opened fire. Their bullets slammed into the brown-clad clean-shaven figure and Toplis was spun around like a cork in a strong-running current.

He went down to the ground and made no attempt to rise. One hand clawed at his middle and blood stained his clenching fingers. Then all movement ceased.

When the police came up cautiously he was dead. The R.A.F. uniform was in the brown-paper parcel with the razor he had used since last speaking to Constable Fulton. Like the Cumberland police constable, he had changed out of uniform to avoid being recognised again, and he had taken time to shave. Possibly, if Constable Fulton had not carefully re-read the description of the wanted man, he might have failed to recognise the man in brown suit and wearing a cap and brown shoes. But Constable Fulton was a first-class policeman.

In the dead man's pockets were several letters from a woman

named Dorothy, who was in love with a killer. But her identity was never divulged. She was the only person in the world Percy Toplis cared for except himself, according to the evidence of the grubby little diary with the short notes and drily humorous comments and a grim last entry—a smear of bright wet blood.

7

THE CASE OF THE BOGUS SUICIDE

NOT very long ago I was involved in a bout of correspondence with a writer from West Berlin who wanted some facts from me about a case I had dealt with in a German publication. In the course of this correspondence reference was made to a number of pre-World War II German criminologists and detectives. One of the latter was Inspector Braun of the city's Detective Bureau.

In return I was given additional details about one of Braun's best performances as a manhunter. It was what I think of as the Case of the Bogus Suicide. It isn't the only bogus suicide case I know of, but it is the only German one. It concerns a corpse identified as that of August Giernoth.

Braun came into the case when he received an official report on what the local police had accepted as a suicide by shooting in a forest some distance outside the then undivided city of Berlin. In the report was the statement that a gun had been found lying near the body. One of the bullets from it had struck the dead man's right temple, destroying that side of his head.

The local police had found personal papers in the pockets of the dead man's jacket. These established an identity. August Giernoth. It had been no difficulty to discover that this man had come from a small town in Silesia, but apparently he had been a failure, and it could have been this fact that drove him to take his life.

At least, that is how things appeared on the surface. The dead man's clothes were worn and not of very good material. He looked uncared for, and there was no money with the papers found in his pockets.

The formal inquest was held, and the coroner ordered the Berlin taxpayers to pay for a modest funeral. It seemed no one regretted Herr Giernoth's passing, not even Herr Giernoth. Inspector Braun swept the few papers on the suicide into a dead file and tried to forget the case of another human who had found the strain of living in the twentieth century thoroughly defeating. However, he was reminded of the filed papers when some short time later another letter arrived on his desk.

It had come from a Berlin bank. Inside was a letter explaining that the enclosed savings deposit book had been left with the bank as security for a loan.

The name on the bank book was August Giernoth.

Braun spent some time fingering that bank book and puzzling why a man who had procured a recent loan from a bank should blow out his brains. To the German detective's way of thinking this was irrational. A man was more likely to blow out his brains when a bank had refused to advance a loan he needed. The other way round did not make much sense.

He went to the branch of the bank that had sent the savings book to police headquarters and asked to see the official who had written the letter. This man said he had read in the newspapers that a suicide's name was Giernoth. It had rung a bell, he had checked, and found that it was the name of the man who had left his savings book as security. The account had been adjusted, and he had sent the bank book to the police simply because he wanted to get rid of it and knew of no other address to send it.

Braun said he wished to check the signature shown in the bank book. Somewhat surprised by this request, the bank official sent an assistant to get the receipt slip for the loan and the original application form which had been filled in when the request for the account to be opened was made. Braun studied the three signatures and decided one was a forgery.

The false signature, Braun decided, was the one on the receipt slip. The signature on the original application form and that on the bank book had obviously been written by the same hand. The one on the receipt for the loan had been written by someone trying to reproduce a similar signature to the others.

"I'd like to know if you have any record of known relatives," Braun told the bank official, who thought the detective was being officious about something that was finished and had been closed in the bank's ledgers.

He was wishing he had refrained from sending the bank book to the police. It was just inviting a lot of official red tape.

However, the bank official was surprised when the record originally attached to the application form was produced. August Giernoth, it appeared, had a brother named Fritz.

"I didn't know," the bank official excused himself, "or I would have sent him the savings book and got a receipt from him."

It would certainly have been simpler, for Fritz Giernoth had an address in Berlin.

Inspector Braun called on him. He brought news to the brother, who was surprised to learn that August was dead.

"You know," he told the detective, "I find it hard to believe August would shoot himself. If anyone had asked me, I would have said, no, he would never do a thing like that. Take his own life? No."

He sounded very positive about it.

Braun watched him closely and when he came to a pause surprised Fritz Giernoth again.

He said, "I don't think your brother did take his own life, Herr Giernoth."

The man he had called on stared at him doubtfully for some

moments until the meaning of the detective's words came to him.

"You're saying you think someone else shot August, Inspector Braun?"

"I'm saying," said Braun carefully, "I think that suicide was bogus. Your brother was murdered."

But when it came to inquiring who might have shot his brother Fritz Giernoth seemed to be of little help. He reminded Braun that his brother was a man who had very little money, and explained that for a long time August had been out of work. In fact, if it had not been for a certain Herr Reimann he might still have been unemployed.

Braun decided he should know more about the man responsible for getting the dead brother employment.

Fritz explained that he himself had been the first brother to come to the German capital from their home village in Silesia, where prospects were not hopeful. He had found a job and set himself up in a couple of rooms, and had then written August that there was more work in Berlin than at home.

August had travelled to Berlin to join his brother, who had made room for him in his own lodging. Fritz, however, had been luckier than his brother in obtaining employment. August tramped from firm to firm without being taken on. He had talked things over with Fritz.

"Why don't you put an advert in the papers?" Fritz had suggested.

August thought it a good idea. They had drafted out what they considered a suitable advertisement together, and August had it inserted in a couple of Berlin newspapers. There had been a reply almost at once. From a man named Reimann.

The man who answered the newspaper advertisement suggested a meeting. This was arranged, and when August Giernoth met Herr Reimann the latter offered him a job as a barman in a hotel with a reasonable wage and the chance of collecting some useful tips from customers.

"August was very pleased about the job. He thought it was

one he would like," Fritz explained to the listening Braun. "But of course he had to provide either a good reference or some means of showing he was a person of substance."

Braun knew very well what Fritz Giernoth meant.

As a barman in a hotel August would be handling money that was his employer's. It was customary years ago in Germany for a newly employed person taking a job with that kind of responsibility to provide a modest kind of bond for the employer, as a sign of good faith and an intention to work honestly. Such a bond would usually be in cash, for which a receipt would be given. Or it could be in the form of a bank book showing a healthy balance in favour of the depositor.

Braun saw how August Giernoth's savings book came to leave its owner's possession in the first place. It had not been handed to the bank by August. Fritz's brother had given the book to Herr Reimann.

"Can you give me a description of Herr Reimann?" he asked the bewildered Fritz.

Here Braun was in luck. Fritz, it transpired, had gone with his brother to meet Herr Reimann, but had not actually been present when the two discussed the terms for August being employed. But Fritz had taken a good look at the man who had answered the advertisement.

Before Inspector Braun left he had written out a very clear description of a man he very much wanted to find.

He began with the filed records of known con men and forgers at police headquarters. It took him several days of turning up possible entries, checking, and cross-checking from other entries, but help came from the slip he had brought away from the bank where August Giernoth had had a savings account. He came upon a specimen of handwriting that appeared to match the writing on the bank slip.

The man whose writing matched that on the slip had a police record. His name was Rudolf Hennig and he was down in the files as a leather worker.

He had been in prison on several occasions, each time on a conviction for theft.

Braun procured a copy of Hennig's filed photo and took it to show Fritz Giernoth, who glanced at it and said without hesitation, "That's Reimann."

The days of patient file-hunting had paid off.

Braun took the photo to the bank that had held the deposit book and the official he had seen before found the man who had arranged the loan and dealt with the payment.

Braun showed the man the photograph. "Do you recognise this customer?" he asked.

"Oh, yes," said the man. "That's August Giernoth."

Getting that answer was a relief to the German detective. He could now ask Rudolf Hennig some very awkward questions. The answers should be interesting, always provided the leather worker with a police record could supply them.

Having arrived at this stage in his investigation, Braun took the fresh file he had prepared to his immediate chief at police headquarters, the Oberregierungsrat.

"I propose asking for a warrant for Hennig's arrest for murder," Braun informed his chief.

When the case he had made out had been considered the authority was given. Braun was also told to call on the Detective Bureau for such help as he required in following up leads to discover the wanted Hennig's whereabouts.

Braun began trying to trace Hennig by assuming that the man had employed more than just the one alias of Reimann. Squads of plain-clothes men threw a dragnet across Berlin. It swept up several criminals who had been lying low, hoping to avoid police attention, but Rudolf Hennig was not one of them. The dragnet operation was continued for a week without the arrest of Hennig.

At a conference held at police headquarters to consider what fresh step could be taken it was decided to give Hennig's photo to the newspapers. The practice of using Press publicity to help in a manhunt was, at that time, less frequently adopted in Germany than in some other European countries. It was considered that newspaper reports were often more helpful in warning a wanted criminal than in bringing needed information to the police seeking it.

So giving out Hennig's photo for distribution among a few million Berliners who regularly bought newspapers was considered to be in the nature of a desperate resource. But the decision taken, publicity was sought with typical German thoroughness. Crime reporters were summoned to police headquarters.

Besides receiving officially stamped copies of the photo the newsmen were lectured on the case, and Inspector Braun attended the briefing to answer questions. When the news conference broke up Rudolf Hennig was about to become page-one's sensation in a number of Berlin and other Brandenburg papers.

What Braun did not tell the Pressmen was his hoped-for result of the big manhunt receiving a great deal of publicity. He wanted to panic the wanted man to run from wherever he was hiding, which was in Berlin, Braun was convinced. If Hennig ran, tried to get out of the city, Braun would have every likely exit covered by men primed with the wanted Hennig's description. Night and day detectives watched at stations and all public transport main depots.

The Press campaign was, in truth, a nine-days wonder—just about. It lasted a little over a week and fizzled out, with no result.

Braun was left feeling he had drawn a complete blank, and it even began to look as though his career had acquired a most unpromising kink. If Hennig was in hiding, as Braun believed he must be, the man was proving too cagey to come out into the open where he could be seen, and he had certainly not tried to leave the city by any normal route.

It was a case of "acting from information received" that lifted the Hennig case out of the doldrums into which it had sunk rather heavily at Berlin police headquarters. Braun was fast reaching the stage where he would be considering the uncomfortable possibility that he had been wrong, and that Rudolf Hennig had indeed got away from the man searching for him, when he was visited by a man who had been a policeman before he had retired from the Berlin force.

The man's first words roused Braun like an electric shock. He said, "I think I know where this man Hennig is, Inspector."

"Where?" Braun asked.

"In my house. I've an idea he's really a man calling himself Hein who rents a room from me."

It was the kind of news Braun had been waiting for. Taking a fresh name and living in a single room was the sort of evasive action he would expect Rudolf Hennig to adopt, especially after reading the newspapers over the past week.

He arranged for a couple of police in uniform to call on this lodger who had given the ex-policeman the name of Hein. They arrived when the man was in, and after opening the door he stared at the callers in surprise. He offered no resistance to accompanying the policemen to a police station, where he suddenly took them by surprise. With a lithe movement he sprang clear of his guards and snatched a gun from a pocket. As the two bewildered men crowded back from him he spun about and raced away.

The angry policemen recovered themselves and ran after him. They were faster, and were catching up when their quarry turned into a tall building and began leaping up the stairs. He kept going to the fifth floor, where he paused to fire a shot down at the men coming after him. Then he jumped for a window and climbed out on to a narrow ledge, where he balanced himself precariously more than sixty feet above a courtyard. There was an alley-way between the building he had entered and the next. It was five feet across. He made his way along the ledge until he was opposite a window in the other building across the space of five feet. Moreover, that window was open. From a crouching stance he leaped over that treacherous chasm between the tall buildings and went pitching headlong into the room on the far side.

It was empty and he piled up on the floor with a sudden wrenching pain in one leg. He picked himself up, limped out of the room and up to the top landing, where he climbed through a skylight he had to force open. He emerged on the roof, to discover a crowd was collecting in the street below and staring up at him.

He commenced running across the roof, concealing himself behind tall chimneys so that the spectators below would lose sight of him. As a cordon of police was spreading out, pushing the crowd back, he darted down through another skylight.

Somehow he eluded the detectives who had been hurriedly summoned and were searching each building in a whole city block and the uniformed police forming the cordon round the block. A reporter on a Berlin newspaper was smart enough to find out how Hennig had worked his impressive disappearing act. His story was printed, and the entire city was suddenly convulsed by an excellent joke at the expense of the police and of the Detective Bureau in particular.

Not the least interested reader of that informative article was Inspector Braun.

He learned that the fugitive had taken off his topcoat and jacket and hat, and hidden them down one of the tall chimneys before returning through the second skylight. In his shirt-sleeves Hennig had limped as quickly as he could down the stairs to reach the shop of a shoemaker on the ground floor. He had turned inside and complained that his shoes were pinching his feet and asked if the man behind the counter could do anything to ease them.

Hennig gave him one shoe and then the other, taking his time while the police search continued. The shoemaker said he would stretch the shoes. But Hennig wasn't satisfied that they were more comfortable to wear until the shoemaker had returned three times to his work-bench. By that time most of the crowd outside in the street had dispersed, and the search by the police had moved farther down the street. Hennig put on his shoes, paid the shopman for his trouble, and walked out into the street unrecognised in his shirt-sleeves and continued on his way past a couple of plain-clothes men who were trying to decide how they had missed the man on the roof.

The newspaper story brought letters from angry readers both to Berlin's editors and to the Detective Bureau. It was a great joke on the police, apparently, until some more thoughtful readers awoke to the fact that a suspected murderer was doing much as he pleased about how he came and went, while the police appeared helpless to detain him.

It was a bad time for Braun.

He was convinced that the killer of August Giernoth had been allowed to escape. So was the Oberregierungsrat. Braun had an unpleasant interview with his chief. When he left the latter's office, however, he had been given authority for calling on the services of more plain-clothes men.

Braun now began to plot a search of the German capital that was prepared like a military campaign. His detectives went over the city district by district. They checked each house in the streets they covered. They took hundreds of statements and accompanied a few uncovered undesirables to police cells.

What they didn't do was come back with Hennig.

Again the wanted suspect had vanished with the finality of a mouse behind a wainscot.

But the great police comb-out provided vast entertainment for the public. Large crowds collected wherever a police van arrived with squads of searchers to go through a fresh area. Not all the entertainment was pacific and tinged with good humour. In one or two instances members of the public seized a man who suddenly ran from a police search and handled him roughly before the police could intervene.

None of the men saved from the crowds was Hennig.

What was happening in Berlin could not be confined to the capital. Newspapers in other German cities printed the story of the intensive hunt for Rudolf Hennig. Reports poured in of the wanted man being seen in other parts of Germany.

Within a few days police all over Germany were hunting a phantom, much in the way British police hunted Percy Toplis when he was the subject of regular newspaper headlines.

However, there was a great difference between those man-hunts. Toplis read the stories of his being seen hundreds of miles away with considerable secret enjoyment. Rudolf Hennig not only enjoyed the fuss he was creating, but tried to stimulate it and earn money by writing about himself for the newspapers who were playing him up as a wanted criminal.

The man who had gone to considerable pains to make a modest sum in marks by killing August Giernoth wrote from his fresh hideout a letter to the *Berliner Lokalanzeiger*. He offered to give that newspaper the exclusive rights to three articles he was prepared to write, describing what had really happened to August Giernoth and to Rudolf Hennig after the bogus suicide had been found by Inspector Braun to be murder.

For the three articles he asked the price of twelve hundred marks, which was three times the sum he had milked from the savings account of the man he had murdered.

In his letter he informed the editor:

"To prove this is not a hoax, and that I am not a lunatic, I enclose the work permit issued to August Giernoth."

He was even sufficiently brazen, by this time, to sign the letter with his own name. At least, the name Braun and the Detective Bureau deemed to be the killer's own—Rudolf Hennig.

As soon as the offer reached the editor of the *Berliner Lokalanzeiger* he got in touch with Braun, who realised the legal importance of the admission it contained. In a roundabout fashion it constituted a confession. Unless the writer was lying in the hope of tricking the paper of twelve hundred marks.

Braun and the paper's editor worked out a reply to the offer which was printed in a prominent position, so that Hennig could not miss it. Hennig was invited to be more specific about the articles and what he would be giving for the price he had named. It was a stall.

But Hennig was prepared to play along.

He sent in another letter, which was largely a repetition of the terms of the first. He was giving nothing away.

After a fresh consultation with Braun the paper's editor inserted another reply in his columns, in which a suggestion was made. If Hennig wrote the first article and sent it to the newspaper's office by messenger the sum of four hundred marks, the price of one of the articles, would be passed over to the messenger in a sealed envelope.

Braun expected Hennig to be snared if he complied.

He was disappointed.

Hennig wrote out the first article, which was no great piece of journalism, and dispatched it to the offices of the *Berliner Lokal-anzeiger*. His messenger was a happy drunk, a porter from one of Berlin's produce markets, who was practically on the point of passing out when Braun's men grabbed him and hastened him to where an impatient Braun was waiting to ask some urgent questions.

The drunk, when sobered up, professed to know nothing about a package he had delivered or the man who had given it to him. But in one of his pockets, when he was searched, Braun had found a cheap notebook, very creased and stained. One page near the end had been turned down at the top corner. On that page had been written the place-name: "Bird of Paradise Tavern, Treptow."

Treptow was a Berlin suburb.

Assuming that the turned-down page and the place-name on it was significant, Braun instructed the dazed porter to return there with the sealed envelope prepared for handing over to Rudolf Hennig.

The man started off, and detectives followed him when he caught a tram to Treptow. From the tram stop he made his way to the Bird of Paradise Tavern.

He did not go inside. He paced up and down on the pavement across the road. Suddenly a man came hurrying up to him, peered at his face and then stopped him.

"You've a letter from the editor of the *Berliner Lokalanzeiger*," the man said hurriedly. "Let me have it."

He held out his hand.

Before the letter could be taken from the market porter's pocket the watching detectives ran up and seized the courier, who proved to be someone Hennig had paid to collect the letter from the porter.

The man was taken to be questioned by Braun, who was beginning to feel thoroughly frustrated by the wily tactics of the elusive Hennig.

The courier's story was that he had been approached by a stranger and offered money to collect a letter from a man outside the Bird of Paradise Tavern. He had been given a description of the man he would meet, and it tallied with the market porter's appearance. He had been sent to the tavern in a taxi, which had broken down, and he had turned up late.

"Where were you to take the letter?" Braun inquired.

The courier explained that he had been told to cross the city to another suburb, where he was to be at a particular street corner at a certain time, when the man to whom the letter was addressed would arrive and take it from him and pay him for his trouble.

Braun decided it sounded fantastic enough to be a true account of how Hennig was operating. Moreover, the man's description of the unknown who had approached him with the offer fitted Hennig.

Braun sent the man on his way with the letter to keep his rendezvous. This second messenger was followed, like the first. He arrived at the street corner on time, and waited. So did Braun's plain-clothes men.

Hennig didn't keep the appointment.

Braun had a conviction that the incredible Rudolf Hennig

was thoroughly enjoying this chasing to and fro across the city, and was deriving a great deal of amusement from how he was making the Detective Bureau's members perform like puppets whose strings he held.

Any lingering doubt the German inspector might have had on this score was removed by a fresh letter that arrived from Hennig at the offices of the *Berliner Lokalanzeiger*. It affected to be severely business-like, giving clear instructions how the money not received for the first article should be sent in another name to a particular post office for poste restante delivery.

"Do we continue?" the editor asked Braun.

"Yes. We can't afford to stop playing his game now," Braun admitted grimly.

So another letter was prepared, addressed to the accommodation name Hennig had given, and a clear instruction was appended: "To be held until called for."

Braun was right. Hennig still had a mind to play games. The courier he sent this time was a schoolboy, who was given the letter, which he took to another rendezvous point. Again the following detectives wasted their time. Hennig did not show up.

Next day the editor of the *Berliner Lokalanzeiger* received a resentful letter from a contributor who still hadn't received his promised four hundred marks. The letter showed that Hennig might not be so amused, at this stage, as Braun had imagined. He wrote like a man with a deep regret.

He regretted not having his four hundred marks.

But he was not making any further immediate suggestions as to how payment should be made. This seeming stalemate lasted for two weary months. Then news came from an unexpected quarter. A policeman in Stettin tried to arrest a thief who had stolen a bicycle, and was fired at. The policeman, however, became angry instead of scared, and attacked the armed thief with his bare fists. After he had arrested the thief he took his violent prisoner to the police station.

That was where the prisoner's identity was discovered.

The bicycle thief was Rudolf Hennig.

Braun took a train to Stettin to collect a man he very much wanted to see. He found Rudolf Hennig to be a man feeling very sorry for himself.

"You would never have got me if that dumb cop hadn't been lucky," Hennig boasted.

"Someone had to be lucky besides you," Braun told him. "And there's always the next cop who's looking for a man like you, Hennig. It had to happen some time."

At the trial the bank savings book, the application form, and the receipt slip were produced, to be haggled over by opposed lawyers. But forgery was established by handwriting experts, and the jury was left with no doubts about the guilt of the prisoner.

After they had brought in their verdict Rudolf Hennig was sentenced to death. He was executed exactly one year to the day after he had murdered August Giernoth.

8

THE CASE OF THE MASKED BANDITS

ON that September afternoon I spent in ex-Commissioner Jean Belin's pleasant garden at Chennevières, besides hearing him talk about Landru and Weidmann and the murders of King Alexander of Yugoslavia and of poor short-sighted Louis Barthou, the French Foreign Minister—all cases Belin investigated—I heard him on the subject of a case that he did not handle.

This came about when he corrected an error on my part.

Apropos of the murders of policemen in England, I mentioned the shootings by Toplis, which occurred some ten years after the Sidney Street seige, which Belin recalled very well. In conversational parenthesis I said that I had a few days before walked across the Place des Ternes, just north of the Etoile, where one of Mettefeu's men was shot down. I made the mistake of referring to Mettefeu as a Sûreté man, like Belin himself, and was hauled up short by some very fast French.

Mettefeu, I was informed very warmly, had been a Préfecture policeman, not a Sûreté man. In short, a Paris local cop, much like the fictional Maigret.

But there was nothing fictional about what was probably Mettefeu's greatest manhunt, one which began and ended with the explosion of firearms, a case notable for one of Mettefeu's men, Inspector Curlier, being mourned as a national hero after he had encountered a vicious cop killer.

Because it was a case Belin remembered vividly he talked about it, and there was good reason for his clear remembrance, for it opened about eight months before Landru met Anatole Deibler for some joint business with a guillotine that took only seconds. Indeed, the opening shots in the Case of the Masked Bandits were fired while the notorious Bluebeard of Paris was living through his last summer in a Versailles prison cell, awaiting the date fixed for his trial, and that depended on the outcome of an intensive investigation being made by Jean Belin in the French capital and out at the Villa Ermitage on the outskirts of Gambais.

Those shots were fired around midnight on a warm summer night in Burgundy.

On the night express from Paris to the South of France two French Army officers had a carriage to themselves. After dinner on the train they had spent the time talking and smoking, until one yawned and they agreed it was time to settle down for the night.

Each curled up in the corner he had chosen and tried to go to sleep to the rhythmic rattling of the wheels on the steel tracks.

Farther down the coach three masked men were opening compartment doors surreptitiously and holding up passengers at gunpoint. They were then relieving them of money, jewellery, and any other valuables the startled travellers had with them, and then threatening with death anyone who stopped the train.

This incredible and boldly conceived robbery had been schemed, and was being carried out, with the care and effrontery of a Jesse James train robbery back in the violent days of America's Wild West.

The time had been deliberately chosen so that the bandits could take their victims completely by surprise and rob them when they were in no position to oppose levelled firearms. The corridors of the train were deserted. The restaurant staff had retired. The bandits met no opposition on their progress down the train—until one of them drew back the sliding door to the compartment where Lieutenant Carabelli and his fellow officer, Captain Morel, were trying to sleep.

As the door slid back Carabelli stirred and opened his eyes. He blinked, as well he might. Only a single low-powered bulb shone from the ceiling of the compartment, but it illuminated the muzzle of a gun in a steady hand, and that gun muzzle was pointed at Carabelli's head.

"Good God," he exclaimed, sitting upright.

His friend awoke and stared. Before he could speak the masked man who had entered said, "Your money, messieurs. Quickly, please."

The pointing gun moved in a short arc and covered Carabelli's friend, who raised a hand to one of the top pockets of his tunic and took out his wallet. He held it out, and the bandit moved to take it. As he did so Carabelli sprang from his corner seat and grabbed at the menacing gun. His fingers closed round the metal barrel, and before the bandit could tighten his grip the lieutenant had wrenched the gun from his grasp.

Carabelli shifted his own grip to the butt, and thrust the muzzle, which he had woke to find pointing at him, against the masked man's throat.

"All right," he said. "You listen to me."

The bandit was quite prepared to do that. In fact, there was little else he could do. Carabelli, by his intrepid action, had turned the tables.

However, the raid had been planned to avoid such a movement on the part of a passenger spoiling the hold-up. What Carabelli had no way of telling was that a second man was outside, while a third masked bandit, also armed, remained on guard lower down the corridor. This last man's task was to cover the retreat of the other two when they left a hold-up compartment with their loot, and to come to their aid if they ran into trouble.

Lieutenant Carabelli was trouble of the worst kind. Meantime the man just outside the compartment had only to glance around the edge of the pushed-back door to see what had happened, and Carabelli's scathing tones told him anything he didn't already know.

He did not hesitate.

He burst into the compartment, pushing past the other bandit, and the gun he held began spilling bullets. Carabelli collapsed before he could squeeze off a shot of his own. In fact, the man at whom he was pointing the gun was lucky not to be shot down by some reflex action of Carabelli's. The lieutenant lay on the compartment floor, blood pouring from his body and spreading over his uniform tunic.

For a few frozen moments the grim tableau remained stationary, a tragedy that had taken all caught up in its swift violence by complete surprise.

It was Captain Morel, the officer who had surrendered his wallet, who broke the immobile group. He forced himself to move and dropped on to his knees beside the sprawled body of the shot man.

"You've murdered him," he gasped.

The killer covered the kneeling officer with the gun he had just used. His companion stooped and caught up the gun Lieutenant Carabelli had dropped as he fell.

"Do nothing," said the killer, his voice thin with menace behind the mask.

The bandits backed out of the compartment. One of them slid the door back. The latch clicked. The sound of the shooting had been almost lost in the noise of the express speeding through the summer night towards Chalon-sur-Saône. But the third bandit, the man left on guard down the corridor, came running up.

"What's happened?" he called. Something had. A single look at the other pair appraised him of that.

"An Army officer got brave," said the killer. "I had to convince him he was a fool."

"How?"

"He's convinced. He's dead."

"So are we if we stop here now," said the third man. He turned and reached for the chain that connected with the train's automatic braking system.

"What are you doing?" said the killer.

"Getting out."

The chain came down with a single sharp tug, and the next instant there was an ear-splitting scream of brakes swiftly applied, and locked wheels whispered savagely over smooth rails as the train began sliding to a halt from about seventy miles an hour.

The bandit nearest a door at the end of the corridor wrenched it open. One after the other the three robbers dropped from the train as it came to a halt and vanished into the darkness beyond the lighted windows. With them disappeared about fifty thousand francs in cash and valuables they had taken from the passengers. They crossed the lines of tracks, reached an embankment, climbed it to a field, and ran across the soft earth silently towards a road.

By the time roused train attendants were crowding into the compartment where Carabelli lay the bandits were scurrying along a metalled road, three grey shadows losing themselves in a pale wash of summer moonlight.

Lieutenant Carabelli was not quite dead when one of the train's attendants told the engine driver to go on to the next station and then stop, but the badly wounded officer was dying. The train ground to a halt minutes later in the next station down the line, and in the stationmaster's room the alarm was raised.

Carabelli was lifted from the train to await the coming of an ambulance which would take him to an hospital in Chalon. When he arrived there the train in which he had been travelling was speeding through the night, heading for Lyons, the Mediterranean, and the Italian frontier, with one compartment door locked and awaiting examination by the police.

There was a pool of drying blood on the floor of that compartment.

Carabelli had been carried to a ward and put in a hastily prepared bed, and was being examined by a night-duty surgeon when he drew his last shuddering breath. Someone at the hospital phoned the local police. A call was put through to Paris and it was switched to police headquarters. A late-duty police officer typed some notes. A copy of them was dumped on the desk of the detective in charge of the Special Brigade in the Préfecture de Police building on the Quai des Orfèvres.

There were follow-up statements taken by police who had caught the train and remained aboard as it headed for the Alpes-Maritimes and the vineyards of Provence after being the scene of murder among the vineyards of Burgundy. These statements had been made by the various passengers who had been robbed. Some contained loose descriptions of the masked bandits, but when read through in Paris the descriptions did not tally. In fact, they were contradictory.

As a means of helping the police the statements were, for the most part, useless.

The man who read through them was Chief Brigadier Mettefeu. He was a man who probably knew more about the habitual criminals of Paris than any other in his time. For this reason he had been handed the case, for the bandits must have joined the train in the capital, and they had planned the hold-up very carefully and with excellent timing, which stamped them as professionals.

It looked very much as though the raid on the Riviera express had been the work of a Paris gang.

Mettefeu had little enough to go on, but he set his brigade members to sifting the Préfecture files for anything that might point to a gang of three men who would set up such a tricky robbery and who would carry it out when armed.

Then Mettefeu caught a train that took him into the vineyards of Burgundy, and he eventually arrived at the place where the train that had been the scene of murder had ground to a stop. It was not very far from Chagny, where the main road to the south is joined by a cross-country road from Dijon and the heart of the Beaune wine country.

He was informed that the local police had been told of a fire that had been lit late the previous night near the cemetery at Nolay. Mettefeu was taken to examine the cold ashes of that fire. He found among them the remains of scorched strips of velvet.

According to the statements sent to Paris the bandits' masks had been wide strips of velvet secured across their faces.

Mettefeu also found in the ashes he raked over burned fragments of leather pocket wallets, scorched papers, and a few fire-blackened trinkets of little worth that had been discarded. Such remains Mettefeu had gathered up and placed in a bag for taking back to Paris.

By the time Mettefeu had finished examining the old fire at Nolay news had been received from the staff at Nolay railway station. Three strangers had arrived in the early hours and had bought three single tickets for Etang on the next westbound train. Unfortunately the man who had sold them the tickets had found no cause to take special note of these late-hour travellers. But the hour was almost five o'clock.

One detail he had observed, for the simple reason that he had not lifted his glance to look at the travellers' faces. The boots of all three had been muddy, as though they had crossed a ploughed field.

Not that muddy boots were unusual in that part of France at an early hour in the morning in what was a farming district.

Mettefeu went on to Etang, where fresh inquiries brought additional news of three men with muddy boots being observed. So far as Mettefeu could find out these men had been making for Nevers, well on the way back to Paris. He went there, and more inquiries were made.

Again witnesses were found who remembered seeing three

men who were strangers walking together, but, as before, no special attention had been paid to them. But Mettefeu did locate a café where they had eaten, and after that time was wasted until he learned that they had most likely moved on in the Paris direction and had headed for Montargis.

Here, once more, the trail was lost until a good many people had been interviewed. Mettefeu was not a man to give up any routine inquiry easily. He kept asking questions until he found someone who was able to tell him such a group of three travellers had moved on towards Charenton, one of the south-eastern Paris suburbs.

There, he knew, he would lose their trail. For Charenton was a terminus of a Métro line. They could take a train and get out anywhere between Charenton and Balard, in south-west Paris, for that Métro line, today designated No. 8, makes a wide loop north of the Seine to turn south again under the Place de la Concorde and head back towards the river not far from Saint-Cloud.

Mettefeu had traced the bandits' route back to Paris, but there the trail vanished at Charenton. The next development could depend on what his men working on the filed records could come up with. He was prepared for a good deal of time to be used up at this stage in covering leads that frustratingly ended in dead ends. But that was specialist work for the Special Brigade, and on balance it was seldom time completely wasted for any inquiry after known criminals of the Paris underworld usually provided a measure of information that would prove useful sooner or later to the men at the Préfecture.

The work of going through the files of known criminals, however, produced no hopeful pointer to the identity of the men who had robbed the passengers aboard the Riviera express.

The one tangible piece of information Mettefeu had about the bandits was that all were young. This fact had been established by the descriptions taken from the passengers who had been robbed. A possible fact, not entirely supported by the statements but certainly hinted at in one or two, was that one of the bandits had been dressed in the kind of clothes that used to be termed sharp.

Not so much a genuine dandy as a would-be dandy—a flashy dresser. This one had worn gloves of a pale grey colour.

From this he deduced that the region that might best pay off in an inquiry would be the dance-hall district of Montparnasse, then, in that year of 1921, enjoying its post-war boom as the favoured haunt of arty types, thinkers who considered themselves emancipated and dressed to demonstrate it, and the gangsters who always flourish where the lamps burn late and not too brightly.

An alternative to Montparnasse was Montmartre, north of the river, an area largely living at that time on a dying reputation as a tourist centre from which the old-time arty types in their cloaks and wide-brimmed black hats had vanished.

The Special Brigade's members covered both districts.

Several likely leads were followed in the area behind the famous Dôme and Coupole cafés, then in their heyday as night-spots, but these petered out. It was a detective of the Brigade, working in the Boulevard de Clichy area of Montmartre, who changed the pace of the manhunt. In a Clichy brasserie he had listened to a young woman named Lucille who had seemed to the detective to be unusually interested in the express hold-up and the shooting of Carabelli.

When he reported Lucille's interest to Mettefeu he said he thought she might be worth his chief's questioning.

Mettefeu was interested to know why a young woman in the north of Paris was excited by the train robbery and murder in Burgundy. It seemed to him that his detective must be right. This was unlikely to be mere coincidence.

He had the girl picked up and brought to the Préfecture, where she adopted a hard-nosed attitude that in itself suggested this was not the first time she had rubbed her smooth young shoulders with the less smooth ones of the *flics*.

"I don't know anything. Not even why I've been arrested," she assured Mettefeu, who told her she was not under arrest, merely being asked to co-operate by telling the police what she knew of the train murder in Burgundy some nights back.

She repeated that she knew nothing.

Mettefeu took this in good part and began asking questions. He was perfectly well aware that she was trying to avoid telling him anything informative, but he was shrewd enough to realise the young woman was being careful to say nothing that could be proved to be an untruth.

It was when Mettefeu began the personal questions that he heard of a man named Guerrier who was currently employed as a bus conductor and was interested in Lucille. He liked attending gala nights at the dance-halls, and on several occasions he had invited Lucille to go with him, and she had been very ready to partner him. Guerrier was good-looking in his way and a ready spender.

Mettefeu turned to Guerrier's friends. He was told about a stranger who had been introduced to Lucille. This second man was a smart dresser, with a broad-shouldered coat, tightly waisted, and glossy patent-leather shoes with pointed toes. He even wore gloves.

"What kind?" Mettefeu asked casually.

"Some sort of grey material," said Lucille. "Anyway, they were light-coloured."

This was the man who had laughed with Guerrier about what he had termed the express job. Guerrier had fidgeted and thrown the other some warning glances, but the man wearing light-coloured gloves had only laughed.

"Cheer up," he had said, as though enjoying a joke. "Next time we won't have just guns. Bombs, Guerrier."

Apparently he had meant grenades. But Mettefeu was both surprised and shocked by what he had learned. For one thing, it was news that there was a gang of criminals in Paris who thought the way, apparently, gangsters were thinking at that time in Chicago and other American cities that had entered the brittle and explosive decade of the Roaring Twenties.

Mettefeu went over her answers again with Lucille, who had become noticeably subdued in the atmosphere of that office which was adjacent to the Palais de Justice and the criminal courts.

"Don't talk about this visit," she was warned before she left.

To make sure she caused no harm by not taking the well-meant advice, Mettefeu had Guerrier picked up within a few hours, when he left the bus depot. He didn't seem scared by being hauled in for questioning, but equally he wasn't happy about helping the police.

He gave a convincing performance of an unhappy man trying to put the best face on things.

He was asked to name his pal with the sharp men's wear and even sharper shoes.

"Oh, that's André," he said.

"André who?" Mettfeu wanted to know.

"I don't know his other name. I met him in a café. We got talking. You know how it is. After that we met a few times."

"What did he talk about?"

"Women, sport, the clubs."

"Did he talk about the train murder in Burgundy?"

Guerrier was silent for a short while, then the story came out in a series of quickly uttered sentences spaced well apart.

André had mentioned the murder and the robbery on the train. He had referred to the hunt the police were making to catch the criminals several times, and he had once said something about bombs for the police in Lucille's hearing. When Mettefeu asked why André should talk about the crime to his café pal Guerrier admitted something he had apparently been unwilling to explain earlier. A short while before the Burgundy train murder André had told him he would soon be reading in the papers about a crime that would have the cops chasing their tails. When Guerrier had asked what he meant he had taken a strip of velvet from one pocket and a ticket to Nice from another. He had put one on the other, and invited Guerrier to guess.

Guerrier hadn't been able to—until later. Then he had been scared, and had warned Lucille about listening to André after he had introduced her to the other man.

Mettefeu produced the bag of charred odds and ends he had brought back from Burgundy. He picked out a piece of scorched velvet and put it down in front of the other man.

"Was this the colour velvet André showed you with the ticket to Nice?" he asked.

Guerrier nodded. He was beginning to look very sorry for himself.

He looked even worse when the next question was put to him.

"Where can we find André?"

There was a lengthy pause. Mettefeu gave the man time. The brigadier could guess what was passing in the bus conductor's mind. The natty dresser was a dangerous man, perhaps a killer. If he found out that his drinking companion had talked about him to the police he might try teaching his friend Guerrier that it pays to keep a still tongue.

On the other hand, Guerrier wanted the police off his back. But it was a hard decision. He made it reluctantly.

"At the Brasserie de la Paix," he said, "in the Rue Cujas."

When he heard that Mettefeu wanted him to accompany some Special Brigade detectives to the café he nearly panicked, but Mettefeu assured him that he would be disguised. The police did not want their best witness recognised.

That evening of July 28th the disguised bus conductor and four of Mettefeu's brigade kept watch on the brasserie. André did not appear. After waiting some hours Mettefeu went inside and questioned the proprietor, who said he did not recognise the description of André. But one of the waiters did. He told Mettefeu that the man he had described had been in earlier and had phoned someone at the Excelsior. The Excelsior was a hotel lower down the Rue Cujas. The phone call for Marcel Bréger, it appeared, had been taken by the manager, for M. Bréger had left the hotel the previous day, the 27th, after staying for a month. No message had been left by the caller on the phone.

Mettefeu asked if this Bréger had left a forwarding address for letters, and was told no, because the man had not given up his room, only left the hotel for a time. In fact, his room was to be kept for a woman who was still in hospital, but would be coming out very shortly. Her name was Mademoiselle Vialle. The manager of the Excelsior understood that she was a very good friend of M. Bréger's.

Mettefeu gave the man a description of André, and after cogitating the manager thought it fitted a M. Cablane, who had stayed at the hotel for one week earlier in the month, and had given up his room on the 5th. M. Cablane had appeared to get along very well with M. Bréger.

"What is Bréger by profession?" Mettefeu inquired.

"A sculptor," he was told and was duly surprised. But he was not so surprised when, on checking, he learned that Bréger had not been in his room on the night of the express robbery. But he had returned the next day, and the hotel manager had noticed that his clothes looked very creased and his boots had mud on them.

Mettefeu asked to be shown the room awaiting Mademoiselle Vialle. He searched it thoroughly, watched by a hotel manager who was becoming anxious at these attentions from the police. Mettefeu found the room was bare of any clues save one, a piece of paper tucked under the strip of carpet by the bed. It appeared to be part of a letter which had been torn across. The part Mettefeu had picked up was a message and had obviously been torn off for reference, then hidden or lost. It read: "Go to the Hôtel de Grenoble and find if Dujardin has returned from Rouen."

Mettefeu went back to the reception desk and asked to see the visitors' register. He found no trace of a M. Cablane staying at the hotel before his recent visit. However, one of the hotel staff, when questioned, said a M. Charrier who had stayed in the hotel about three years before had looked very like M. Cablane. M. Charrier was quite young and had been a medical student.

With this last piece of information Mettefeu seemed to arrive at the end of a most hopeful lead.

He went back to the Préfecture and had the records of the Service des Garnis searched. These records contained the names of hotel guests reported when they booked in. He found the Hôtel de Grenoble, but its guest lists contained neither the name Cablane nor Charrier. On the other hand, he came across a Dujardin.

Gaston Dujardin had, he perceived, booked into the Grenoble on the day following Cablane's exit from the Excelsior. It seemed neat enough to be very interesting. A fresh check with Préfecture files of convicted criminals turned up blanks for Cablane and Dujardin. But a Jacques Mecislas Charrier, who was twenty-six, having been born in Paris on May 2nd, 1895, had been to prison. His photo was taken from the files and shown to the manager and staff at the Excelsior. Two persons who looked at it said the photo was of Cablane.

Mettefeu went through the same procedure at the Hôtel de Grenoble, with a curiously similar result. There Charrier was again recognised—but as Dujardin.

Mettefeu was really in luck by this time, for he was told Gaston Dujardin had entered wearing his pale gloves and carrying a walking-stick only minutes before the brigadier's arrival. Instead of arresting this man of various names, Mettefeu waited to discover if Marcel Bréger contacted him. A long night's wait of the kind Belin had undergone in the Rue de Rochechouart two years before was lived through impatiently, but no Bréger turned up. In the morning when Charrier left, wearing his light gloves, he was arrested. In his pocket was an automatic with a full magazine. In the hands of the police he became vociferous and admitted that he had two accomplices, Thomas and Bertrand. The latter was Marcel Bréger. At the Préfecture he picked out their photos and confessed to meeting them in jail, where they had planned a robbery in Marseilles, which had been easy, and then had planned the train robbery. Arrangements had been finalised on Friday, July 23rd. The leader of the enterprise, Charrier claimed, was Thomas.

After a whole day's search the two wanted men were found to be sitting at a table on the pavement outside a café in the Place des Ternes. Two of Mettefeu's men who had tracked them down took places at a table only a few feet away. More members of the Special Brigade took up positions around the wheel-hub of busy streets. Suddenly the watched men rose, one threw down some money for the drinks, and they started to walk away fast. What had alerted them was never known. Mettefeu's men jumped into action to prevent the quarry getting away. It was a show-down. The wanted men reached the Avenue de Wagram, one of the spokes of that wheel-hub, drew guns, and began shooting. The detectives fired back. Thomas fell dead on the pavement. Bertrand spun around, wounded badly, and as he went down shot four bullets into Inspector Curlier. Bertrand and Curlier both died within seconds of each other.

Charrier remained, the only one of the deadly trio to stand trial for the famous hold-up and murder. Before the trial opened the dead Curlier was posthumously awarded the Légion d'Honneur. The day he was buried the streets of the route were lined with spectators paying homage to a brave policeman who had served his fellow-citizens well.

Charrier's trial was notable for the prisoner's contempt for the officials and the proceedings alike. When asked by the president of the court for his name he replied, "The bastard Mecislas Charrier." When he spoke to the jury it was in defiance: "I am neither mad nor unbalanced. I claim entire responsibility for all my actions. I am a desperate enemy of society and my hatred will only end with my death. I defy you, gentlemen of the jury, to take my head."

The jury accepted the defiant challenge and on August 22nd, 1922, Anatole Deibler claimed that head on their behalf.

9

THE CASE OF THE CARDBOARD SQUARE

I REMEMBER talking to the late Fred Cherill about his most notable murder cases on the occasion of his becoming a member of a certain luncheon club. At the time we had been discussing some writing he had been asked to undertake.

"Which would you say was your most interesting case?" I put to him.

He gave me that familiar owlish look and his slow smile came and went as he said in his slightly ponderous way, rounding each word before it left his mouth, "I don't know that I would want to single out any particular one, but if I had to, I think I'd say helping Bill Chapman land George Russell was as big a challenge as any."

It is the murder I think of as the Case of the Cardboard Square. On the most remarkable fingerprint evidence provided by a painstaking Cherrill in that case a callous killer was convicted and later hanged.

The Yard's Murder Squad team that worked on the case comprised the late Superintendent Bill Chapman, the pipe-smoking sleuth who unravelled the problem posed by the Luton torso mystery, and his assistant, Sergeant Hislop. They entered the case on a Wednesday. The date was June 2nd, 1948, and the first intimation Scotland Yard had that one of its Murder Squad teams was required in Berkshire was when the county's Chief Constable picked up the phone in his Reading office and rang the Commissioner of the Metropolitan Police.

It wasn't long after that call had been put through to the old Whitehall 1212 number that Chapman and Hislop set off for Maidenhead. Hislop carried the much-publicised "murder bag" containing the team's tools of the detective trade. Chapman was a bit broody. The victim, he had been told, was an old woman of ninety-four.

Her death hadn't been easy. It had been, as a matter of fact, particularly brutal, having regard to the poor old soul's age. Chapman smoked his pipe on the journey to Maidenhead in a moody silence. He had no fondness for people who knocked defenceless old women about.

He arrived at Maidenhead feeling grim.

What he found waiting for him did nothing to make him feel better about this new murder case.

The pair of Yard detectives were met by Superintendent Crombie of the Berkshire Constabulary. He had ready the details that would put Chapman in the picture with no loss of time.

The dead woman was a Mrs. Freeman Lee, something of a recluse, as she had a right to be at that advanced age. Each morning the milkman left her a bottle of milk, but the previous day the milk roundsman had become alarmed at finding two days' bottles still on the step. To the roundsman, whose name was Rome, it seemed very likely that something had happened to the old girl who lived in this rambling large house called Wynford. But he wasn't sure that he should leave the delivering of his milk to make a report. After all, she could have gone away and forgotten to tell him or leave a note. Elderly people are forgetful.

While he was debating the best thing to do he heard the sound of wood being sawn. It came from the next garden. The roundsman walked to the fence and looked over. A man in his shirt-sleeves was sawing a plank. He was actually making a caravan for the summer holidays.

"I say," called Rome.

The man stopped sawing, looked up, and asked, "Something the matter?"

Rome held up the bottle of milk he had brought to Wynford. "The last two days' milk is still on the step. Do you know if Mrs. Lee's still at home?"

The neighbour building the caravan was Arthur Hillsdon, a man of friendly disposition, with time to help someone in a dilemma.

"Just a minute," he said. "I'll come round there."

He walked round into the next garden.

"I don't think she's gone away," he told Rome. "Let's have a look in her bedroom. She sleeps on the ground floor."

With the roundsman following him he walked to a ground-floor window and peered into the room beyond, which was old Mrs. Lee's general living-room. He could see her bed in a far corner, and the table where she ate her food. The room was, in effect, a cell where she lived through the hours of her life, morning and night, a woman who had lived long and was content to ask little of her life's twilight.

The neighbour from next door then walked round to the front door, lifted the letter-box latch, and peered into the hall. He remained staring through that small slot as though at a peep-show, for in the hall were some cushions on the floor and a black travelling trunk secured with a strap. Near the trunk was a woman's shoe. It lay on its side, looking very out of place. So did the bunch of keys he noticed when his eyes travelled over the hall floor again.

He moved back from the door and turned to the waiting milkman.

"Something looks wrong. There's no sign of her. I'd better tell the police."

When the police were notified they got in touch with a local solicitor, Kenneth Ruffe Thomas, who was known to be a personal friend of the elderly occupant of Wynford. Mr. Thomas agreed to go to the house with a police constable, and not long afterwards he arrived at Wynford with Constable Langton. When their knocking brought no response the solicitor told the policeman they had better force open the door.

After the door had been prised open the two friendly intruders looked in the rooms upstairs and down without finding the elderly Mrs. Lee. They went into the garden and began looking behind shrubs and trees. They came back without finding her.

At first glance it looked as though Mrs. Lee might have had the trunk packed for dispatch before leaving, and then had left without sending it on. It was barely possible she might have been so forgetful.

But it was extremely unlikely that she would have left that shoe lying in a discarded fashion in the middle of the hall. And she certainly would not have left without her bunch of house keys.

Yet she had seemingly vanished.

The solicitor walked back into the hall. He moved to the strapped trunk, and said to Constable Langton, "Give me a hand opening this, constable."

The strap was undone and the trunk's lid pushed back. Inside was an assortment of old clothes that had been tumbled in no sort of order into the trunk.

The constable said, "I'd better report to the station, Mr. Thomas."

While he was phoning the solicitor walked again to the musty-smelling old trunk with the pile of clothes inside, and stirred the assortment of cardigans and skirts and blouses, and suddenly he stood very still.

In a nest of other stale-smelling clothing lay an arm.

The solicitor removed some more clothes and found Mrs. Lee. She was dead and her grey head had been battered. Her thin arms had been dragged behind her and knotted together with a shawl. A handkerchief that had obviously been used to gag her had slipped from her mouth and hung around her neck. There were no shoes on her feet, but the other shoe of the one left lying in the hall was with the clothes that had been stowed on top of the old woman's body.

Mr. Thomas could not help feeling nauseated by sight of the kindly woman he had known for a good many years being tossed like a broken doll into a pile of old clothing. There was something so contemptuous of human life about this bizarre discovery that he felt terribly angry, as did the Yard men when they arrived to take over at Wynford from Superintendent Crombie's men.

By then Chapman had been filled in on the old woman's background.

Obviously she had lived longer than most of her friends and, apart from some persons like Mr. Thomas, she knew relatively few people and had almost never gone out during the past year. She had been the wife of a successful barrister, and in a distant past the Lees had entertained a good deal. But for Mrs. Lee the bright world she had known clouded over when her favourite son had been killed in the First World War. Not many years afterwards her husband had died. That was when she ceased to take any great interest in what happened outside the gates of Wynford. From time to time she had consulted her closest remaining friend from the dead past, Kenneth Ruffe Thomas, who had known her husband and been the good friend of both. He advised her on various legal matters that intruded from the outside world, and at intervals bore witness to the changes time wrought in her, as when she had to take to hobbling about with a stick after a partial paralysis had made walking a great burden. Then she had retired to her one cell-like room.

There had been a break of a few years, during World War II, when she had gone to live with another son and Wynford had been let furnished. But after the war she had spoken of returning to the house she thought of as her home. In 1947, despite her family's pleas not to go back, she had made a return that was in the nature of a pilgrimage to the past.

So far as the police could discover the last person to have seen her alive apart from her killer was an electrician who arrived at Wynford in the evening of May 29th to fix up a boiling ring for the old woman.

The post mortem was undertaken by Dr. Keith Simpson. The well-known Home Office pathologist had considerable difficulty in establishing a time of death. He could say with greater certainty what was the cause of death—shock following upon the severe blows to the head. He determined, however, that there had been a lapse of time between the attack on her and the moment she ceased breathing. Her last expiring moments ceased through actual suffocation.

The implication of this was clear. Although unconscious, Mrs. Lee had been alive when rammed into the old trunk with the armfuls of clothes to cover her.

The day after Chapman and Hislop went down to Berkshire Superintendent Cherrill followed them from London. He took with him his portable case, which was a fingerprint laboratory in miniature. It closed up like a small but bulky suitcase, and was carried by a leather handle. The contents were ingeniously contrived neither to rattle nor spill about in motion.

It was a little more than ten years since he had found the famous stocking print in the Wimbledon lover's lane murder, back in July 1938, and he entered this case on the same day of the week, a Thursday. In the decade that had elapsed a great many changes had taken place in the Yard's Fingerprint Department, of which Fred Cherrill was now in charge. Most of the changes were the result of his own ability to organise and improve.

Although he was a big-framed man, stocky and somewhat ponderous of manner, Fred Cherrill was a dynamo of energy so long as he could operate at his own pace. I remember on one occasion when I visited him at his home in Mitcham, soon after he had retired, being shown his workshop in the garden, and some massive pieces of furniture he had made. The results looked like the handiwork of a professional joiner. Cherrill liked using his hands. He used them at Wynford. He went over the whole rambling house, which at first glance had caused his spirits to flag. For upon arrival he found himself confronted by seventeen rooms under Wynford's roof, and he knew the score. In one of those seventeen rooms, possibly in some out-of-the-way place, there could be a fingerprint that he had to find.

Actually he didn't find a fingerprint to help him.

Only a small part of one single print, to comprise, in his own words, "one of the greatest triumphs in the realm of fingerprint detection."

He started on the ground floor, where the old woman had lived for the past year since her return to Wynford, and in that cluttered-up room where she had spent her days and nights he began with the table in front of the fireplace. There was the remains of a meal on it. Close by was an armchair piled with cushions, and at the far side of the room a single bed, the pillow still holding the impression made by a sleeper's head, the bedclothes tossed to one side. There was another table in the room, and this held the remains of a bottle of very flat beer, a teapot, a clock, some glasses, and a bowl of fruit that was withering in the summer heat. A third table, pushed against a wall, was much smaller than the others. This held the old woman's radio, and in front of it was a London evening paper dated several days previously.

There was other furniture in that over-crowded and musty room. A sideboard was covered with small pieces of chinaware, and the exploring fingerprints expert came upon pots of preserves, tins of coffee and packets of salt, old-fashioned soup tureens, condiment sets, as well as an out-dated china basin with matching water-jug. It was a room dull-glazed with poverty. This was a hard fact, as it transpired, for Mr. Thomas was able to tell the police that at the time of her death Mrs. Freeman Lee had no personal resources and almost no monetary reserves, and was living on a modest allowance made to her by a legal benevolent society.

So much for what had been concealed by the imposing façade of a wide seventeen-room house that occupied a wide corner site between Ray Park Avenue and Ray Park Road, Maidenhead.

Cherrill went over every object in that room, leaving the bed till last. When he reached it he felt himself on a quest that was proving singularly frustrating. That half-finished bottle of beer had looked hopeful, to say the least. He had drawn blank with it.

When he tugged the bedclothes away and folded them in a neat pile he felt himself merely going through routine motions. He gathered up the eiderdown to fold it, and something fell to the floor. He dropped the eiderdown and stooped to pick up what proved to be the bottom of a small cardboard box, not more than a couple of inches square. He examined it through his lens, noting the texture and sheen of the material. He found indications of that glazed surface being fingered recently, but his lens could not define actual print impressions.

He may have been hoping for too much, he felt, as he was about to put the small cardboard square down on a table. But then he had a curious feeling, amounting almost to what is meant by a hunch, that he might have a key to this case in his hands. It was a sharp sense of awareness that he had known on previous cases, and he was never able to explain. It was like some subtle sixth sense coming to his aid. He stood there staring at the cardboard square, unable to do anything except empty his mind of conscious thought. That was when he suddenly put down the piece of cardboard that had been the bottom of a box and began searching for—the lid.

He refolded the eiderdown, placed it on the pile of bedclothes, and started a fresh hunt for another piece of cardboard. He found it under the bed. It had been trodden flat. Removing it with his forceps, he dropped it on a fresh sheet of paper and examined it through his lens for prints. On the extreme edge of one side he found what appeared to look like some sort of impression, but rather small.

He knew he had found what he had come from London to

find. He knew because, at very first glance, his experienced eye saw that the part-print it had found had not been made by the woman who had lived in that room.

He carefully packaged this piece of crushed cardboard, which was the lid of a small box that had come from the United States, and continued with his coverage of that large old house so badly in need of a fresh coat of paint and new wallpaper. He worked for hours, but at the end of a thoroughly exhausting day his total of useful findings was that crushed piece of cardboard and the part-print it held. He did not even find any worth-while fingerprints on the black trunk or its strap or the shoe.

Cherrill returned to London with his fingerprint case and the square of cardboard that he sensed was important. At the Yard the tiny marks he had found on the box top were photographed. When these were enlarged and returned to him he saw that, as he had thought, they were part of a finger's or a thumb's print. This left him with a sizeable problem.

How could he discover from which single print these marks had come *if* the whole print was among the millions on file at Scotland Yard?

When it came to considering which finger, he had first to decide which hand, and then which part of a finger. Cherrill had some ten million or so prints to choose from as a start. But when one considered how many sections of a finger's print had to be compared, to make sure these marks he had found belonged in a complete pattern, the possible permutations were rather frightening. Allowing a possible five positions on each print for conceivable comparison, then there were fifty million possible comparisons. It was the kind of figure astronomers were used to, not a working detective.

Fred Cherrill was a cigarette smoker. That was a moment when he felt he needed a smoke. He lit a cigarette and pushed his chair away from his desk. He wanted to stop being a detective and try putting himself in the place of whoever had made that small portion of a single fingerprint. He began by imagining he had just killed a fragile old woman and wanted to be out of the house with anything of value he had pocketed, and he had stopped to pick up a small cardboard box with a label bearing the name of a firm in Fifth Avenue, New York. He reached out a hand to open the box and noted how he would have held it—diagonally by the corners.

But the murderer had not done that.

He began trying to perform a natural way of opening that box to provide a partial print just where he had found it. He did not succeed until he found himself using the thumb and third finger of his right hand. The partial print then appeared to correspond with the part of his right-hand third finger that touched the edge of the cardboard square.

He put the lid down, pushed aside an ash-tray littered with dead butts, and picked up his phone. He asked his assistant, Chief Inspector Holten, to join him, and when the chief inspector entered explained what he had done and what he wanted Holten to do—start checking their files by a known right-hand ring-finger formula. Holten collected the enlarged photo of the part-print and left.

Cherrill lit a fresh cigarette. He was still smoking it when Holten came back, looking excited.

"I've got it," he announced.

He put on the desk before Cherrill a set of prints he had taken from the record files. Cherrill took the enlarged photo from Holten and compared the ridge marks on it with the third finger of the right hand in the set on his desk. He saw that the part-print fitted the ridge marks of the whole print perfectly in exact correspondence. There could be no question that the complete prints of the man who had made that fragmentary fingerprint on the lid of a box in Mrs. Freeman Lee's room at Wynford were those on Cherrill's desk.

Cherrill looked at the man's name.

It was George Russell. He was a convicted housebreaker and thief with an unenviable record.

His fingerprints had been placed in the Yard's files some fifteen years before, back in 1933. They had been found, at that time, on the emptied till of a public-house in Oxford. He had been convicted because he had left them behind. In the intervening years he had lived the life of a small-time crook.

He had seen the inside of several jails. Now he had suddenly moved into the big time.

He was a wanted murderer.

Yet he had tried not to leave his fingerprints in the house where he had killed an old woman and desperately hunted for valuables that were not there to be found. George Russell had doubtless heard of the recluse who lived alone. He had stood outside the front gate and looked at the big house through the trees and told himself a place like that smelled of money. He felt he had come upon easy pickings.

Because he was essentially a small-time crook he had been unnecessarily brutal, relying on strength to defeat an old woman who could have been a very small obstacle to a determined thief who used his head instead of his brawn.

Cherrill returned to Maidenhead. He found Chapman, still making routine inquiries with his sergeant, and feeling all the time he was a man in a cul-de-sac that led nowhere. He needed a brand-new lead.

He received it when Cherrill walked up to him, his mouth kinked at the corners and a tell-tale light in his eyes.

"You've got something, Fred?" Chapman asked.

"His name, if that'll do."

"Nice going. He's got a record, then?"

"Long enough. His name's Russell. I've brought his photo and record."

The first stage of the case was closed. Chapman's manhunt was about to begin the second stage. The superintendent organised a major dragnet to collect a man who had had ample time to disappear into some far corner of the land and lie low. But Chapman was an old hand at operating a manhunt on a big scale. He used the Press, every police force in the land, and turned his dragnet across lodging-houses, institutions, workhouses, poor men's clubs, Salvation Army hostels—anywhere that a man wanting to lose himself might turn to in the hope of avoiding recognition and capture.

The whole operation was one integrated and very intensive search of high operational quality. Even farms with isolated barns were on the list to be covered, woodlands where a man could conceal himself like an animal, disused quarries, old car dumps. Given time that search would have systematically covered every likely place in England and Wales. It might have taken weeks, but the coverage would have been complete.

As it turned out, the search lasted five days.

George Russell was discovered living in an institution at St. Albans. He had been doing his best to avoid attracting attention, and had been congratulating himself on being missed by the police when he was tapped on the shoulder and asked to accompany a detective.

When Chapman saw him the Yard man started cautiously. He didn't want to create difficulties for himself, for he could guess very well that an old hand like Russell would have a story ready to tell.

He was right.

Asked to account for his movements just before that Tuesday when Mrs. Lee was murdered, and for the twenty-four-hour period of the fatal day, Russell went back to May 28th. He said he had been in Maidenhead and had done some work for a woman in the town. When he had finished she had paid him and he had gone to the Berry Café and had a meal. Afterwards he had set off for a drink and had turned in at the Gardener's Arms. In the public bar he had started up a conversation with a couple of men, father and son, named Stock. When he left the pub he made his way to Old Windsor, where he arrived in time to find an old shed, in which he had spent the night. The next morning he had started off towards Staines.

On the Sunday, May 30th, which was the day after the electrician had called at Wynford in the evening to fix the boiling ring, Russell insisted he had gone out hymn-singing in the streets. The canting humbug claimed to have collected a pocketful of coppers from sympathetic passers-by.

Chapman asked if he had any way of establishing his claim to have been elsewhere on the day of the murder.

"You can ask the people I've told you about," Russell said.

"You haven't covered the day of the Maidenhead murder," Chapman reminded him.

"Well, I can't remember where I was every day. I was moving about, living rough. I've told you."

It seemed to the Yard man that Russell had his own reason for not wanting to talk about the day of the murder. He could guess what it was. Russell was scared of being tricked in a lie that could be proved was not the truth.

He had pretended to be above board, but only up to the danger date.

Chapman tried other tactics.

He held up a scarf which Russell had taken to the St. Albans institution. Chapman had done some checking, and knew as an established fact that this scarf had been the property of the dead woman.

"Where did you get this?" he inquired casually.

Russell gave him a look and stared at the scarf. He ran a darting tongue over dry lips and risked a lie.

"From a man I met in a Salvation Army hostel," he told the Yard man with a very open and honest look on his not too clean face.

Chapman nodded and put the scarf aside. The lie would be of value later. He had his next question ready, one Russell couldn't forestall or dodge.

The Yard man asked, "Have you ever been in Mrs. Lee's house in Ray Park Avenue?"

Russell's tongue went back behind his yellow teeth.

"No."

It sounded like indrawn breath twisted into a word.

Chapman explained how he knew Russell had lied. He was at pains to make sure the suddenly quivering tramp in front of him understood the full weight of the evidence. It was when Russell heard of how he had left enough of one fingerprint for Fred Cherrill to work out his identity that he appeared stupefied and defeated.

But even in moments when he was thoroughly scared he did not confess to the crime. He somehow managed to get a grip on himself and said he wished to make a fresh statement. Chapman had a new collection of half-truths and lies taken down. Russell made a great point of not being a man who would harm an old woman.

Somehow it never got close to sounding convincing, and the man who was now a prisoner seemed to realise it. Russell had played his last card, and it wasn't good enough.

He heard himself formally charged with Mrs. Lee's murder a short time later, and eventually he was tried for that crime at the Berkshire Assizes.

His counsel, Mr. Eric Sachs, boldly attacked the testimony of Cherrill and Chapman. The superintendent was challenged about the statement taken from Russell in St. Albans, because it sounded too much like police evidence. Such phrases as "I proceeded," Mr. Sachs claimed, did not sound like the prisoner. He argued that they sounded more like a policeman writing up a statement.

Unfortunately for this shrewd thrust, the effect was spoiled almost comically when his counsel put the prisoner in the witness box and Russell "proceeded" everywhere he went.

It was obvious that it was a phrase Russell had picked up in his regular appearances in police courts.

Mr. Sachs was even more thrustful in his attack when he had Fred Cherrill in the witness box under cross-examination. He produced a textbook diagram drawn to large scale and asked the fingerprint expert to look at it. Cherrill stared at it and recognised an enlarged drawing of his own. He informed the defence counsel why it looked familiar to him. Mr. Sachs was taken aback, but still asked Cherrill to demonstrate the characteristics of fingerprints. However, at no stage was he able to extend his challenge to cast a reasonable doubt on the validity of Cherrill's identifying the third finger of the prisoner's right hand.

The jury listened attentively. They had every reason to. They were listening to testimony by an expert that was in every way quite unique in the annals of murder trials.

When Mr. Justice Hallett summed up he told them that he felt compelled to take notice of the fact that during the trial "a great attack had been made upon Superintendent Chapman and his collegues."

The jury retired and came back with a verdict of guilty.

The prisoner listened to the judge sentence him to death by hanging without being aware that he was gripping the third finger of his right hand with his left hand.

Possibly it had come to him, rather late, that he had helped to make criminal history by giving Fred Cherrill a chance to demonstrate his brilliance as an expert in his own field of finger-prints.

Russell was hanged a few weeks later, without setting the seal on Cherrill's achievement by confessing.

10

THE CASE OF THE DISAPPOINTED ARTIST

JOE MENDELSOHN was one of the footsloggers who helped to create the world-wide reputation of the famous Pinkerton Detective Agency, whose badge became a sign manual known all round the globe. It was a wide-open eye, with the boastful legend, "We Never Sleep."

Boastful but true, nonetheless.

As the Case of the Disappointed Artist demonstrated in full measure. It was a murder case that was investigated under the direction of one of the agency's top men of his time, Superintendent Bangs, who had been with Allan Pinkerton in the days when the Scots-born Chicago detective was breaking through to national fame.

The case opened, for the record, on a cold Sunday in March, when the good folk of the New Jersey town of Edgewood were walking to church. Standing in the middle of a roadway was the familiar figure of their local constable, looking very perplexed and like a man who had no very good idea of what to do next. As a matter of fact, he hadn't. He was a man who knew how to deal with petty thefts and with tramps who sneaked into a barn for a night's rest and left in the morning with whatever they could lay their hands on. He had no experience of handling murder, and was suddenly very aware of the fact.

He was the local law, responsible for handling a grim discovery. A beaten-up corpse, naked except for some under-garments, had been found lying on the fringe of a wood just outside the small town, which was really not much more than a village. The centre of the town was the church, and there was a street of shops and stores, and the Gross Hotel was probably the most imposing building, apart from the church, of which the Edgewood citizens could boast.

The constable sought the coroner. The corpse, that of a young man from first appearances, was removed from the unseemly position it occupied, in full public view, at the time it had been found.

When cleansed the corpse presented a sorry spectacle to the frowning gaze of the coroner. For the man, a stranger to the district, had been felled by a heavy blow on the back of the head. Presumably it was when the victim had fallen that the killer had stabbed the body several times just under the heart. The stab wounds were not of great depth, and the stabbing weapon could have been a pocket-knife. But whoever was responsible had been intent on committing murder. For the victim had been dead when the knife was used.

As a consequence the body wounds had bled but little.

The coroner held his formal inquiry, but there was virtually no informative evidence to be taken. The jury listened to the brief medical testimony, and provided the verdict expected of them. The citizens had the responsibility of setting in motion the legal machinery that would bring a murderer to justice. They were not a little awed by the prospect.

For one thing, the small town was but a short distance from teeming New York City. Most of the working Edgewood males commuted daily to the big city, which had daily newspapers that ran to big headlines when murder was committed, especially one that was in any way spectacular.

And that word certainly described the corpse dressed only in under-garments. The fact that the discovery had been made on a Sunday, almost at church time, somehow seemed to add to the horror of the crime.

A few of the town's prominent citizens met to discuss the best way of handling an unsavoury situation that could bring a good deal of unwanted publicity to Edgewood. Thomas Sharples, a lawyer whose home was in Edgewood, took the lead in summoning this meeting and expressing a forceful opinion about what was required to be done.

"We ought to do something as a community to make sure this murder is dealt with effectively," he told them. "We can't afford to leave it to the county authorities."

"Why not?" someone wanted to know. "The sheriff is responsible for handling crimes of violence."

Apparently the lawyer, who had had occasion to work with the county's law enforcement officers in the past, was not impressed by the prospect of how they would perform in the present case.

"They're not used to handling murder," he pointed out. "We want experts in crime detection to handle this case, get it cleared up for us. If we don't, and if the New York papers get hold of the story and play it up, that could be a bad thing for Edgewood."

There was no disagreement on that point. Sharples was asked what he proposed, and the lawyer showed he had been giving the matter some thought by immediately providing an answer.

"Bring in Pinkerton's," he said.

"That'll cost money," he was reminded.

"Sure," he agreed. "But we can collect enough to pay for some action, and if we leave it till later there will be less chance of getting the murderer caught."

It was agreed that, in the interests of their town, the men who had listened to the lawyer would back his proposal to apply for help from the famous Pinkerton Detective Agency provided Sharples could get the approval of the local deputy sheriff. The latter was smart enough to realise if the private detective agency found the murderer some of the credit must rub off on him. On the other hand, if Pinkerton's fell down on the job, then he could easily dissociate himself with a failure.

He agreed that the town should do what the responsible citizens felt was best in the circumstances.

Sharples wrote a letter to the agency.

It arrived on the desk of Superintendent George Bangs, who was then in charge of the agency's field work. Bangs himself had won an enviable reputation in the United States by his own performances as a detective, and also as a secret agent working for the Union during the Civil War. He was a man who could be compared to John Wilson Murray, his contemporary and head of the Criminal Investigation Bureau in Ontario. The two men had much in common as detectives with international outlooks, as men experienced in the techniques of their day, and as successful career operators who had risen to the peak of their profession.

Bangs' office at the time he received the letter from Thomas Sharples was at a famous Pinkerton address—66 Exchange Place, New York.

When he read what the Edgewood lawyer had to say he made a typical decision. He went personally to the small town instead of delegating the visit to one of his first-rate operatives. Possibly he realised that the town could not avoid some publicity of a startling and sensational kind. If the Pinkerton name was associated with the investigation into the murder, then the man responsible for the agency's image in the east of the United States wanted the publicity to be favourable.

He arrived in Edgewood and saw Sharples after he had taken a room at the Gross Hotel.

The first thing Bangs wanted to know was if the victim had been identified since Sharples had written to Exchange Place. The answer was no. Bangs was starting at the beginning. Nothing was known that could help him, nothing had been discovered.

He went from Sharples to the deputy sheriff, and made sure he would get co-operation from the local authorities and not opposition. With that important detail fixed to his satisfaction he was taken to look at the body.

His first impression was that the face was Nordic, probably Teutonic. Well, there were plenty of Germans in the New York area, for Bangs was already convinced that the corpse had not come to be dumped on the edge of this small town by mere coincidence. He felt that proximity to New York City had meaning in this case.

The body was that of a young man who had been quite good-looking in life. Bangs was interested in the victim's hands. He knew hands were a useful index to what a man does or what he has been. The first thing he noticed about the dead man at Edgewood was that he had not been employed in heavy manual labour. There were no rough patches of skin or callouses on the slim, tapering fingers with cared-for nails.

The deputy sheriff, who was present during Bangs' examination of the victim, asked the Pinkerton superintendent what he found to interest him in the hands.

"Their appearance," Bangs explained. "He certainly didn't use them at heavy work. I'd say they look like the hands of a professional man. However, there's no noticeable pen callous, so perhaps he might have been an artist."

To the local deputy from the sheriff's office this sounded a rather fancy deduction. It certainly wasn't one he would have made. He watched Bangs turn to the under-garments that had been taken from the corpse.

"Don't think you'll find anything there to help, Mr. Bangs," he said. "I've gone over them."

Bangs nodded, accepting the reassurance, but he still examined the underclothes. Again he became interested. First, in their quality and texture. The socks were of wool and he thought they could have been German made. The long-johns or leg-length woollen pants were certainly of American make, but the undershirt seemed to him foreign. It was on the undershirt that he found the nearest thing to a clue.

He detected a kind of outline that had been made in the material. It was a pucker mark, as though someone had stitched something to the material and then released the stitches after the outline had been impregnated on the undershirt. The something could have been another piece of material, like a badge, which would have been distinctly unusual. Or it might have been the stitches of some embroidery that had noticeably puckered the surface of the undershirt on the left breast. Embroidery suggested possible initials.

Bangs flattened out the undershirt, and tried to trace the faint pucker lines created by the threads that had been withdrawn from the fabric. He found, to his surprise, he was able to trace with reasonable clearness two initials.

A.B.

Assuming that the killer of this unknown man who might have been an artist had removed the embroidered initials, then their removal could only have been made to make identification less easy. This suggested A.B. were the dead man's initials.

Bangs also considered the implication of those unnecessary stab wounds, made with a short-bladed knife. Either they had been made by a killer who was a sadist, in which case Bangs would have expected more carving up of the body, or they pointed to a man with considerable hatred for the victim. In short, a killer who had been unable to restrain the violence of which he was capable.

The deputy sheriff produced a bloodstained length of wood, which had been found not far from the body. The wood was smoothed and shaped.

"It's a barrel stave," the local lawman informed him as he saw Bangs studying the unpleasant relic. "Not much question in my mind that it's what was used to break his head, Mr. Bangs."

Bangs was in agreement this time.

When the corpse was sheeted over again Bangs left the small room feeling that the killer had been someone who hated or feared a man whose initials were A.B., who had killed from such motivation, and had then been sufficiently shrewd to decide which was the best way of getting rid of a corpse in a hurry, and at the same time had realised that denuding the body of top clothes and shoes, as well as that fancy monogram on his under-shirt, would hamper any investigation following the finding of the dead man. The killer, to Bangs' mind, was a coldly calculating person who would not be deterred by seeming difficulties and would not shrink from violence.

A dangerous person, by any normal standard.

He went back to his hotel and phoned his office at Exchange Place. He gave his staff a description of an unknown whose initials were most likely A.B. The man was youngish, might be German and so have a German name. His hands suggested an artist.

"Circulate this to all our offices," he instructed, "and then have an advertisement placed in the *World*."

He read out the advertisement he had prepared. It appeared in the following day's New York *World*, which was the paper mostly favoured by German emigrants and newcomers to the United States.

The advertisement read:

"Information wanted about German artist, aged about twenty-eight, initials A.B., who came to this country within the past few months and who has for more than a week been missing from usual haunts."

After the advertisement was a box number. Anyone reading it would have no reason for supposing a detective had inserted the request.

Bangs was back at Exchange Place when a reply to the advertisement was forwarded from the *World* offices. It was a letter from a man named Jacob Kuenzle, who lived in the Yorkville area, which had a large German colony. He intimated briefly that he thought he knew the young man referred to in the advertisement.

Bangs went to see Jacob Kuenzle. He found him to be an elderly man, quiet-mannered, who showed him a spare key he had in his pocket.

"This is Adolf's," he said.

Apparently he thought the young man in the advertisement was Adolf Bohner, who had lodged in the same apartment house. He had become friendly with the young man, who had given him his spare door key to mind, as he had put it, "in case I happen to forget to go out with mine."

"I'd like to see inside his room," Bangs said.

He received a strange look from the other man. But Jacob Kuenzle was a man who had learned how to restrain his curiosity. All he said was, "Very well. I will come with you, Mr. Bangs."

The two went to the apartment of the missing Bohner, and Bangs found himself staring round a modest room that seemed to be kept neatly. There was a faint film of dust on things. He crossed to a tallboy and pulled open a drawer. Lying inside, neatly stacked, were a pile of shirts and underclothes. Bangs turned over the undershirts. Each had a neatly embroidered monogram on the left breast.

The clearly defined letters of the monogram, in a Gothic script, were A.B. It was fashioned in identical outline with the puckers he had noticed on the undershirt in Edgewood.

Bangs suddenly knew, with deep satisfaction, that he had come a long way by accompanying Jacob Kuenzle up to this room in Yorkville.

The elderly friend of the missing Adolf Bohner had perceived Bangs' interest in the stitchwork and mistook the reason.

"Adolf's fiancée embroidered his initials on his vests before he left Germany."

"Where did he live in Germany?" Bangs inquired, putting back the undershirts on the pile from which he had taken them.

"Strasbourg."

It seemed a piece of stark irony that the Pinkerton superintendent should be standing in that small room in Yorkville listening to the story of a young man who had come from Strasbourg, in Europe, to end up dead and almost naked in a small town in New Jersey, just across the Hudson from the city where he had arrived in the New World.

Bangs realised he must tell the patient Jacob Kuenzle the truth. The man had been helpful. He might be even more so in helping to trace a murderer.

So in his young friend's room the grey-haired man heard that young Bohner, whom he had taken to, had been brutally slain and his body left on the edge of a wood.

After he had recovered from the shock of the Pinkerton man's news the other gave Bangs one fresh piece of information that did not come as a surprise.

"Adolf was an artist, Mr. Bangs, but he could not sell what he painted. He went from one dealer to another, but they would not consider handling the work of a young and completely unknown artist. I'm afraid he was terribly disappointed. He had come to America to make a fresh start. He thought here he would be accepted and he could make money which he could send to Rosa for her passage to join him."

"Rosa is his fiancée?"

Jacob Kuenzle nodded. "But Adolf told me of another man who tried to win her affection away from him in Strasbourg. That was why he wanted to get money to send for her so that they could be married."

It sounded like the dream of all the world's separated sweethearts. Bangs was not a sentimental man. He worked at a job where sentiment had no room except occasionally in a witness's testimony. But he was touched by the curious element of pathos he seemed to be uncovering in the story of the disappointed artist who might also have been a disappointed lover.

When he sounded out Jacob Kuenzle on this point the grey-haired man shook his head vigorously.

"Oh, Adolf was sure his Rosa would remain faithful to him while he tried to get a start here in America," he told Bangs.

Bangs switched to Bohner's new friends since his arrival from Europe. He was told that Bohner had lived rather quietly since he had taken his room in the apartment house. He was also informed that the elderly friend he had made knew of only one visitor who came to visit the disappointed artist. This was a dark-featured man with a small mouth.

"A man I would not trust," Jacob Kuenzle said simply.

Bangs had crossed to a small desk in the room. He looked through it and found a diary with entries in German. He asked the other man to read out a few. He heard a few random opinions about New York and some home thoughts about Strasbourg, nothing about people.

"Turn to the last entry," he said.

Kuenzle ran his eyes over it and said in English, "Must go to New Jersey tomorrow and get that business settled."

"Let me see," said Bangs, taking the diary and glancing at the date of the final entry.

It was the Thursday before the Sunday when the body was found by the wood. Three days before. Hardly of value as a clue at that moment.

Bangs returned to Exchange Place. He cabled the Pinkerton representative in Strasbourg. The cable went in the Pinkerton regular code.

He received a reply in the same code. It informed him Adolf Bohner came of a respectable family that had suffered financial reverses. These had resulted in the son leaving an art school and going to America to make a fresh start. He had a fiancée named Rosa, who still considered herself engaged to him. However, prompted by Bangs' original cable, the man in Strasbourg had made further inquiries and had learned of a man of not such a good-standing family as the Bohners who had courted Rosa without success. He was August Franssen, of Bohner's age, the son of a shoemaker. Instead of joining his father at shoemaking, he had sought adventure and had become a pikeman in the company of Swiss Guards retained by the Vatican. Bohner and Rosa had become engaged while Franssen was in Italy. When Franssen returned to Strasbourg Bohner had suddenly decided to try his luck in New York. He had left almost on the spur of the moment. Very shortly afterwards Franssen had vanished from Strasbourg. So had his father's life savings.

Bangs drafted a fresh cable to Europe. In it he asked the man in Strasbourg to procure and send him a photo of August Franssen. The Pinkerton superintendent had a feeling about the shape this case would take from here on.

When the photo arrived from Europe he showed it to Kuenzle. He was keenly disappointed when the grey-haired man shook his head over it and confessed he had never seen the man before.

"Isn't this the man who visited young Bohner?" Bangs asked.

"No, Mr. Bangs."

It was a firm negative. Bangs couldn't get round it and he didn't try. But he tried for more information about the man Kuenzle had seen, and it was with a show of diffidence that the other admitted being aware of a smell in the room where he had been introduced to the dark-faced man.

"What sort of smell?" Bangs pressed.

"Rather like leather."

If Jacob Kuenzle had not been an incurious man he might have asked Bangs why he smiled. Bangs did not explain that he was thinking a man freshly arrived in New York without money would most likely find a job at a trade he knew something about. August Franssen had not wanted to be a shoemaker, but the chances were he had tried his hand at it before deciding to don a medieval uniform and plumed helmet and parade with a pike.

The search began for Franssen. Bangs sent one of his best men, Harry Brockman, to Edgewood. He put up at the Gross Hotel and started cautious inquiries. He came up with nothing. Then Bangs cabled Strasbourg again, this time for Rosa's news of

Franssen. The reply was a rebuff. The girl said he was in Alsace and sometimes returned to the Rhine city. All he could do was send Brockman back to Edgewood with intructions to widen his field of inquiry. This time Brockman did better. He found a shoemaker named Heinkel in a town some distance from Edgewood who had hired a young worker named Arthur Francis who spoke faltering English. Not only were the initials those of August Franssen. So was the general description.

Bangs had Brockman check with the photo. This ended in a fresh setback. For Heinkel said Francis looked nothing like the photo. For one thing, he had a moustache and wore glasses.

Bangs took heart from the fact that Franssen could be good at disguising himself. If he was, then Rosa had lied. Another cable to Strasbourg suggested putting pressure on the girl and threatening her with intervention by the German police. The threat worked.

Rosa admitted lying because she was scared of the questions put to her. She said August Franssen had followed Adolf Bohner to New York, and she had not heard from him since he sailed.

Bangs now put to work on the case Joseph Mendelsohn, a Pinkerton man who had been born in Germany and even worked at shoemaking for a time. Mendelsohn started inquiries in the Yorkville district of New York. He began buying foremen at shoe factories a midday beer. He soon heard of Franssen, who had borrowed cash from workmates and left before paying it back. He also heard of a girl who had been friendly with Franssen. She had gone into the country to take a job on a farm. He traced her and made her angry simply by mentioning Franssen's name, but she calmed down and told him he might find Franssen at a saloon in Forsyth Street.

When Bangs was told he ordered Mendelsohn to keep after the wanted man.

So Joe Mendelsohn took to hanging around Forsyth Street. A week passed before August Franssen returned to the saloon, just as the angry girl had said he would. Mendelsohn followed the man from the saloon to a shoe factory. He reported again to Bangs, who told him to make friends with Franssen.

"Win his confidence if you can, Joe," Bangs said.

Mendelsohn was found a job in the factory where Franssen worked after some secret Pinkerton strings had been pulled, and the detective had no difficulty in placing himself in a position where he could lend Franssen a small sum. It was a short-cut to friendship, but being friendly didn't induce Franssen to talk about himself or his past. Joe Mendelsohn began wasting a lot of time, as it seemed to him, but there was no short-cut to a withheld confidence.

Brockman, still in the Edgewood district, turned up a valuable clue. He heard from Mrs. Heinkel that Francis had been friendly with a local girl, whom he sought out. She said she hadn't seen Arthur for some time, not since he had given her the gloves she was wearing. They were not new, Brockman saw, and were really a man's pale buckskin gloves. He pretended to admire them. That was when he saw the not-quite-eradicated initials on them.

The familiar A.B.

Brockman also stopped at an inn well off a main road, where he learned of a man who had said he was a shoemaker and who had been provided with supper on the Saturday night before the finding of the body at Edgewood. The general description could fit Franssen.

Next it was Joe Mendelsohn's turn to report. He had loaned Franssen more cash to enable the latter to travel out to the West, and in return had received some articles Franssen was anxious to dispose of. These included a pawnticket for a suit of clothes. The suit was redeemed, and when the jacket and trousers were shown to Jacob Kuenzle he said with no hesitation, "That's Adolf's suit."

Mendelsohn was ordered to set up the arrest of the young man anxious to travel West, as though following Horace Greeley's famous exhortation.

Accordingly he arranged to see Franssen off at the ferry on the morning the latter was planning to leave New York and head for California. The arrest was a close-run affair, and Joe Mendelsohn had a bad time, for Franssen overslept, and then the other Pinkerton operatives did not appear, and Mendelsohn had to stall by suggesting he was ready to change his mind and join his friend. The ferry's whistle was being blown, and Franssen was breaking into a run for the pier, when George Bangs, who had been delayed in procuring the necessary warrant, and other familiar faces from Exchange Place appeared.

Franssen fought like a man in a frenzy to get clear, and did not subside until the handcuffs clicked around his wrists. The timing was as tight as any closing scene in a TV crime drama.

Bangs tried to get Franssen to admit that he had killed Bohner because he had hated the other man for winning Rosa while Franssen was in Italy. But Franssen refused to discuss the girl or talk about Bohner.

So the case came to court with the Pinkerton Agency not being able to provide the prosecution with a signed confession, which would have made the proceedings much more simple and direct. Franssen fought them in court every inch of a long, long way, and they had to marshal all the evidence they had procured before the trial closed with the man charged being found guilty and sentenced to death.

But Franssen cheated the executioner.

His legal advisers asked for a retrial on the grounds of a technical error in the trial procedure. They were granted a retrial.

At the second trial the Pinkerton Agency's evidence was paraded again, and for the second time it sufficiently convinced a jury to bring in a verdict of guilty. But this time the finding was accompanied by a recommendation to mercy, which meant automatically the substitution of life imprisonment for execution.

So August Franssen stayed in North America, but he did not reach California's sunshine.

Nor did he return to Strasbourg and to a girl named Rosa.

It is not known how Thomas Sharples and his friends in Edgewood felt when they received the Pinkerton Agency's bill for their work on the case. It isn't even known, outside the Pinkerton ledgers, what that bill amounted to.

But the good citizens of Edgewood had no reason to complain of not receiving value for money. Their small town had become an integral part of a true-crime classic.

11

THE CASE OF THE WHITE FEATHERS

Trinidad, like a few other regions in the West Indies, is a veritable human melting-pot. In most Europeans' minds it is associated with the production of three basic exports—oil, asphalt, and calypsos. It is also an offshore island off the coast of Venezuela, from which it is separated by the Bay of Paria, and is geographically dead north of the gaping mouths of the Orinoco River. It is a self-contained land with a waterfall which is a tourist sight. This is the Maracas Falls, from which name the semi-dumbell-like percussion and rhythm-pounding instruments of the steel bands and Latin combos take their name. It has several volcanoes which erupt mud instead of lava.

Not surprisingly murder is not unknown on the island.

It is a land of heat and at times of tension, both personal and political. The crimes that occur there seldom make headlines in another hemisphere. One that occurred in the close warm spring of 1954 did.

In April of that year a fisherman in Godinot Bay saw a bulky object that had apparently been washed up on the sandy shore of the small inlet with the big-sounding name. He went closer to inspect the object, and found it to be a tied-up sack. When he opened it damp sand tumbled over his brown hands. He cleared the sand away and peered inside.

Then he wished he hadn't.

The sack was inhabited—by a corpse which should not have been there. Furthermore the corpse was that of a woman. To make things even worse, she was a white woman.

Or she had been.

The fisherman left what he had found and ran back to his boat. He was in a hurry to tell someone of his discovery.

Godinot Bay is rather less than forty miles from the island's capital of Port of Spain, an old-time buccaneer's anchorage and rendezvous with a colourful history of blood and danger and chests of booty and doubloons. It is naturally, in these days, the centre of the island's police network. The fisherman's find was reported to police headquarters there, and the man who received the news was Superintendent Reid.

Jeffrey Reid called to his chief assistant, Lieutenant Clark, who came in and received the news with a solemn look, as well he might. This was the kind of treasure trove Trinidad could well do without.

The two police officers drove out to Godinot Bay without any delay, and arrived at the place where the gruesome sack still remained beyond the lapping waters of the Caribbean, watched with suppressed excitement by a crowd of local villagers who had collected as soon as word of the fisherman's find had circulated in the neighbourhood. The superintendent began his examination, a not pleasant task, for the action of the sea and the moving sand had worked to spoil the dead woman's looks. But from what he could see of the remains Superintendent Reid was sure she had been young. Her limbs had the appearance of a young woman's. They were slender and still retained an ocular suggestion of suppleness.

"I think we can decide we've got a murder on our hands," the superintendent told his assistant. "But we'll have to have a post mortem to be sure."

After all, whoever the woman was, she might have died of natural causes and her death proved such an embarrassment that someone had decided to dispose of the body furtively. It was unlikely, but unlikely things do happen, and Trinidad is the kind of place on the map where unlikely events can be expected to occur more frequently than in a good many larger places.

Superintendent Reid knew that very well.

He also knew that with its heterogeneous and extremely mixed population of black, yellow, bronze, and white faces the possible combinations of violence are numerous. He felt this was certainly one.

Which meant the police would have to find the person responsible for putting the woman in the sack. Then there would be a murder charge.

In any case, the body of a white woman found in a sack on the seashore was going to mean newspaper and radio interest, for Trinidad is a tourist centre. The police would most likely have to work hard to take up this challenge and answer it. But of course, as Superintendent Reid realised, it had not been planned for the police to be challenged. The woman was merely to disappear. The sand accompanying her body in the jute bag was obviously to weight it so that the sack would sink with its burden.

But Caribbean tides are as unpredictable and fractious as tides elsewhere. This wasn't the first time the sea had surrendered something intended to be lost conveniently for ever. There was the notorious case of a torso that had been surrendered by the sea in Australia, while an incoming tide in Essex had brought back human remains that resulted in Brian Donald Hume standing in the dock at the Old Bailey accused of murder, a man who is currently in jail in Switzerland for another killing. This time on dry land. Moreover, he is likely to stay there, for the Swiss are as salty and matter-of-fact as their own Emmenthal cheese. They believe that life imprisonment should mean what it says it is.

The body that had been cleansed of the gritty particles of wet sand was transferred to the nearest town, which was San Fernando. There it was taken into the building which was the local mortuary, to await the arrival of the district's medical officer, Russell Barrow, who had spent two years in post-graduate work at King's College Hospital, in Gower Street, London.

Superintendent Reid did not feel disposed to return to Port of Spain without knowing the result of Dr. Barrow's examination, so he and Lieutenant Clark remained in San Fernando until the post mortem was completed.

The investigation, when it started, would have to go into top gear. Moreover, it would be another case of the police starting from scratch. For no one had sent in a report of a woman missing from her home.

In the circumstances this not only appeared strange, but looked decidedly ominous.

When he had finished his examination Dr. Barrow put on his coat and came to look for the two waiting police officers. He looked grave.

However, he had finished only the first part of the complete post mortem, or a first examination, as it were, for he had found himself confronted by a curious problem.

The woman had been strangled. That meant murder as Jeffrey Reid had correctly decided when he first looked at the sack's contents.

But the victim had been in the sea for a number of days. How many Dr. Barrow could not say at this preliminary stage because he had another factor to consider, one which complicated everything he did at the post mortem.

As he said to the appalled police officers, "She was literally eviscerated."

In short, the internal organs had been removed. This horrific act could suggest anything from voodoo to a Jack the Ripper quality of animal sadism. The expressions on the faces of the superintendent and his assistant showed enough of their feelings at this news to reflect Dr. Barrow's grave thoughts. This was going to sound bad whichever way it was told or reported.

He informed his attentive audience, "A six-inch incision was made to clear out the intestinal tract." He promised to give them a full report as soon as he was able.

The two men from police headquarters had got what they had waited for, anyway, confirmation of murder. The butchery apart, someone had first strangled the woman. Her death had been caused by strangulation. The knife work had been a gross refinement in addition to the act of murder.

The police officers left assured by the doctor that the evisceration, on the evidence of what he had seen on the slab in the operating room of the mortuary, could have been undertaken by anyone who had fundamental medical knowledge and understood anatomy. He even reminded them that such a job could have been done by anyone used to gutting livestock.

Reid returned to Port of Spain conscious that he not only had a murder case on his hands, but a messy one at that. He found the town alive with rumours. It had become general knowledge during his absence that the police were looking into the murder of a white woman who had been brutally treated before her body had been sacked and thrown into the sea, like so much garbage.

Dr. Barrow, however, completed his work at San Fernando sooner than he had anticipated. He came to police headquarters primed with has latest discovery. He had found that the victim was young, as Reid had originally supposed. He put her age at somewhere between twenty-five and thirty. His opinion that she had been strangled, and that strangulation had been the cause of death, had been confirmed by his closer and more detailed examination.

But there had been more evidence of butchery.

For instance, the victim's jugular vein had been slashed, like a pig's, to bleed the body and drain away the veinous blood. This savage act had been committed, as he had discovered by examination and tests, before the abdominal incision had been made and the intestines removed.

Dr. Barrow had had to perform the grotesque task of cleaning quantities of sand from the corpse's orifices, especially those that were unnatural in every sense of the word. He had also sifted the sand remaining in the sack with the doubled-up body.

When he had removed the sand from the mouth he had found in it a gold filling from a tooth cavity. This he placed in front of Reid. He put down beside the glinting little cone of gold a tinkling charm bracelet of the kind that was fashionable at that time. There was also a medallion that looked as though it might have been a luckpiece.

"I found these in the sand in the bottom of the sack," he explained.

"Was she blonde or brunette?" the superintendent inquired.

"Blonde," the doctor told him.

"That the lot, doctor?"

Dr. Barrow nodded, and then caught himself up.

"Oh, there is something else," he said. "I thought it rather surprising, as a matter of fact."

He paused as though considering his next words carefully, staring the while at the objects he had laid out on the desk in front of Jeffrey Reid, who waited for what was to come.

"I was still engaged on the most mortem when Dr. Singh came in."

"Dr. Singh?" Superintendent Reid sounded surprised.

"Yes. You know him, I suppose?"

"Indeed I do. He has a practice here in Port of Spain. What was he doing out there?"

Dr. Barrow considered his reply in the same way as before. He seemed uneasy.

At last he said, "Well, he said he had come to borrow one or two of my textbooks. But he gave me the feeling that this was only an excuse."

"For what?"

"To see the body."

Reid frowned. He was very anxious to get this clear.

"You're saying, doctor," he said slowly, "that Dr. Singh, in your opnion, came into that room where you were performing the post mortem so that he could find out whose body it was?"

Dr. Barrow shook his head slowly.

He said just as slowly, and in a very unhappy voice, "He gave me the impression, superintendent, that he knew whose body it was."

The two men, doctor and police superintendent, stared at each other. What had just been uttered could hardly be retracted, and Dr. Barrow realised that just as certainly as the man who had listened to him.

Reid eased back in his chair. He looked down at the pieces of shaped metal on his desk as though he expected them to provide him with a silent answer to his thoughts. At last he lifted his gaze to the doctor's face.

"You'd better tell me what you know about Dr. Singh," he said quietly.

The Port of Spain police chief knew quite a deal about Dr. Dalip Lutchmie Persad Singh already. He knew that the Hindu doctor was the son of a couple who had come from India to settle in Trinidad thirty years before. They had arrived like many other hard-working Orientals, indentured to a family as servants. They had saved their wages, invested those savings carefully, and had finally been able to bring up a family of three children and educate them. Their son Dalip was the child of whom they had the highest hopes. They had provided the money for him to go to Scotland to train as a medical student and take his doctor's degree. As many Hindu parents do, they had planned his life for him, if not precisely from the cradle to the grave, at least from the cradle to the nuptial bed. They had chosen the doe-eyed Hindu girl he was to come back and marry when he could set up in the island as a doctor. But Dalip Singh had learned a few things in Europe his parents had forgot to warn him against. He had taken his degree, become the doctor of medicine his parents wanted him to be, but when he returned to Trinidad he did not arrive back with only his clothes and a new set of scalpels and forceps. He brought a bride.

She was a German girl.

Dalip Singh had solved the alleged colour bar for himself by stepping over it.

His parents had been very upset.

So had Dr. Barrow's sister Lucy. Superintendent Reid had guessed at the reason. Now the doctor proceeded to explain something he had not told anyone before. He had no alternative in view of what had happened.

As the superintendent knew very well, Dr. Barrow had come to know Singh in Britain, but when the two doctors returned to Trinidad they rarely met. In fact, it seemed that both took precautions not to meet. There had to be a reason.

Her name, as the doctor explained quietly, was Lucy Barrow.

She was the doctor's sister, and she had journeyed to England to be with her brother and his wife during part of their two-year stay in London while Russell Barrow was studying at King's College Hospital. She travelled by sea, and it was on the voyage that she met the smiling Dalip Singh, on his way to study medicine in Edinburgh. What occurred with a background of wild waters and possibly an Atlantic moon hanging in the sky like a lantern was the kind of chemical attraction that is customarily explained away by the word romance. Something very liable to happen and flow between good-looking young people of opposite sexes. Even between not so good-looking older people of opposite sexes who should know better.

For such atmospheric romances are notoriously short-lived. Not all, but most by a very considerable majority.

Lucy Barrow was an exception to this shipboard rule.

In Port of Spain she would hardly have noticed a stranger named Dalip Singh, and it would probably have been unthinkable that she could have considered herself falling in love with the smooth-featured Hindu. But for days at sea, living almost in a suspended dream state, the chemical attraction worked its profound magic. She arrived in Britain with news for her brother

She was thinking of marrying Dalip Singh, who was going to Scotland to study medicine and become a doctor.

Apparently, from what was explained by her brother in that room where Superintendent Reid sat listening to a very human, and in some ways rather touching story of bewildered youth, she had not changed her mind in the passing months. It had been changed for her—by Singh marrying a German girl named Inge.

The new Mrs. Singh had returned to Trinidad with her husband. They made a striking pair, the dark good looks of the very white-smiled Hindu contrasting sharply and effectively with the golden paleness of his Nordic wife. In the circle to which she was introduced socially on the island Mrs. Singh became immediately popular. She talked brightly, she had charm in addition to good looks, and she was a most friendly hostess with a recipe of her own which won acclaim.

This was her speciality drink, ananas-bowle. As the first word suggests, it was a concoction based on pineapple juice, but the native rum of the West Indies, as well as some champagne and a dry white wine gave ananas-bowle a distinction that was both merited and appreciated.

Further, Mrs. Singh was a professional woman. She was a woman with diplomas as an optician, which allowed her to supplement her husband's medical service. She had, in fact, enlarged her own professional activities to include an optician's practice on three other islands, Grenada, St. Lucia, and St. Vincent.

Mrs. Singh, as a career woman, was a notable success in her new Caribbean setting.

Whether she was an equal success as a wife was, very naturally, less easily established. She had certainly provided, perhaps innocently, a contretemps for the Barrows while they were in London. She had been taken to visit them by Dalip Singh, who had not only introduced her to Lucy Barrow, but had told her that he was engaged to the German woman.

In view of what had taken place, it was understandable that

Dr. Barrow had very mixed feelings about his Hindu fellov
medico in Port of Spain. However, feelings are not evidence, an
the superintendent clearly had to take a look at the obverse of th
medal. He made some notes about what he had been told an
Dr. Barrow took his leave. The result of the post mortem he ha
conducted would be kept in the official files. The next statemen
quite obviously, would have to come from Dr. Singh, whos
curious insistence on going to see the body on which Russe
Barrow was performing an autopsy certainly required explair
ing.

Always assuming that Dr. Barrow was correct, and that th
excuse of borrowing some textbooks was no more than a
excuse. In any case, it was a most inconvenient time to choose
ask for the loan of books, and there were libraries on the islan
where the books could have been procured.

However the arrival of Dr. Singh during the course of the po
mortem was considered, it appeared odd to the point of bein
perhaps compulsive. As though the Hindu had not been able
deny himself the visit at that particular time.

Superintendent Reid asked his assistant to call on Dr. Sing
and request him to look in at police headquarters. The lieutena
had no trouble finding the Hindu doctor. He was at home, ar
he readily agreed to accompany Lieutenant Clark there ar
then.

So it was not very long after Dr. Barrow had left him that D
Singh was shown into the office where Superintendent Reid s
at his desk. He wore a large pair of sunglasses, which gave h
dark face a mildly sinister appearance and concealed the brigh
ness of his intelligent eyes. Almost as soon as he entered the offi
the sunglasses were turned towards the metal objects on tl
superintendent's desk. The superintendent could imagine, fro
the seeming concentration of that gaze, that the concealed ey
were very wide.

Perhaps with shock.

The police chief said quietly, "There's the unidentified bo

of a woman in the mortuary at San Fernando. These objects belonged to her. Can you help us with identifying them?"

The man who was staring at the displayed charm bracelet and medallion took a deep breath and his shoulders seemed to sag, but he found the words to reply after a short struggle with his feelings.

"They are my wife's," he told the superintendent.

Reid then inquired where Mrs. Singh was.

"I wish I knew," the Hindu doctor replied.

"When did you see her last?" Reid wanted to know.

Dr. Singh did not have to think about that. He answered readily, "On the sixth of April."

But he seemed to be holding himself in, trying to control warring emotions that could make him go to pieces in front of the quiet efficiency displayed by the police superintendent who was watching his performance with close attention.

He was invited to tell what had happened on that date.

After a short pause he told Reid his wife had walked out on him that night. He told no one because he had been anxious to avoid the spread of gossip that could be malicious and damaging. In any case, he insisted, he knew she would return to him.

But she still had not come back when he heard that a white woman's body had been found at Godinot Bay and that Dr. Barrow was undertaking a post mortem on it at the San Fernando mortuary. He had gone there feeling anxious.

He paused again in his explanation, and then added, "But it didn't appear to be the body of my wife." Then he once more insisted, "She'll come back. I know she will."

It was not a very satisfactory performance, and the man who made it must have been aware that he would be expected to answer questions that would help clarify his position.

The questions came. Superintendent Reid wanted to be told more precisely why the doctor's wife had walked out on him. Was the reason a quarrel, and if so had another man been the cause?

But Dalip Singh shook his head and in a rather obstinate tone told the listening superintendent that there had been no quarrel with his wife. Then he added words that were supposed to explain an apparent caprice.

"It isn't unusual for her to go off like this," he said. "She's always been the victim of periodic depressions. At these times she wanted to be on her own."

It was very weak.

The moment had arrived for shock tactics. Reid assured him that the blonde woman whose body had been found in the sack was his wife, and then thanked him for looking in so promptly and wished him good-day. After another quick glance at the objects arrayed on Reid's desk the stooping shoulders of Dr. Singh turned away and the man walked slowly out of the office.

Superintendent Reid was in a somewhat delicate position. The island of Trinidad was small. When he moved he had to advance with certainty in this murder case. There was no room for experimental manoeuvring.

He was somewhat surprised when he spoke to Dr. Singh's parents. The Hindu mother made no effort to conceal her pleasure at the news that her daughter-in-law was dead.

"She should be dead," she said in a voice that strangely did not sound as callous as her words. "She was no good."

It appeared that the elderly Mrs. Singh had considered the younger Mrs. Singh too free in displaying her undoubted physical charms. The skirts she wore were too short, the dresses cut too low. Inge Singh had been a wife lacking in the modesty expected of a Hindu married woman. For being herself, a European liking European current female fashions, she was condemned.

East was condemning West.

Apparently the twain had met, but not with a happy marital result.

Reid and Clark left the home of the elderly Singhs and went to another part of the city, where their son's houseboy lived. His name was Kramchand Ramsahaye and he was a quick-eyed East Indian. He had a place to sleep in a shanty occupied by a family named Boyeur and he appeared to be a lively, intelligent lad. He had no hesitation in telling the police visitors that he had no liking for his blonde mistress, whom he described as cruel, a woman who always shouted at him and had sometimes smacked him with the flat of her hand. He had no respect, as well as no liking, for her. Largely because she drank to excess.

According to young Ramsahaye Dr. Singh had married a drunk.

It began to look and sound as though Dalip Singh had not been so wise in his choice of a life partner. But that was no excuse for murder, or the world would be full of slaughtered alcoholics.

Reid was told by the East Indian that he had recently been given notice by Dr. Singh, whom he referred to with almost affection in his voice as Uncle Doc. Asked when he last saw Mrs. Singh, Ramsahaye said April 6th. The date, according to the husband, when his wife walked out on him because she was depressed.

When Reid learned that the Boyeurs had sold fruit to the Singh household he asked to speak with them, and Enid, the wife, told him something that surprised him. She said she liked Mrs. Singh.

"Did she hit you?" Reid asked, and that was a question, he found, that neither Enid Boyeur nor her hsuband George, who had worked as a gardener for the Singhs, would answer.

The Boyeurs had a son who had helped his father in the Singhs' garden. Suddenly Ramsahaye pulled up the boy's shirt and pointed to a long weal on his back.

"So you like her?" he flung at the mother sarcastically.

Reid felt he was up against a strange conspiracy of some kind. Lieutenant Clark felt the same when he learned that some ten days before her mutilated body arrived on the beach a pattern of white feathers had been furtively placed on the doorstep of the Singhs' home.

Inge Singh had taken, apparently, no notice of a native voodoo sign, for the feathers had been plucked from a chicken. A white cockerel is a bird often sacrificed in voodoo rites.

Reid was suddenly more convinced than ever that it behoved him to proceed with extreme caution. Some of the Trinidad newspapers had editors who felt differently. There were editorials hinting that the police were dragging their feet in the case and trying not to involve some persons in a bad scandal. The truth was that Reid and Clark were making intensive inquiries in the native quarters, trying to learn if there had been someone employing voodoo spells against the murdered woman. The complexion of the murder was contradictory. The blood-letting and stomach-emptying could point to voodoo, but not strangulation.

A day over a month after Mrs. Singh had left home, according to her husband, on May 7th, a note in a pencilled scrawl was delivered to police headquarters. It read:

"I want to tell you that you are on the rong track. Mr. Don Bain was he come gave me £100 to help in the job. He give me only £30. That night Mr. Bain carry me to a house in Marli St., he a white man they call Doc with glass on he eye and the next man they call Ches bring the bag in a car P1020. I sorry for Dr. Singh he is not guilty. Mr. Ches take the bag in the boat to Godinot then put him in schooner. I today give back the Dr. Singh the passport and bracelet."

This near gibberish did not throw a couple of experienced policemen out of their stride. As Reid said afterwards, "It stank."

Two more days passed before Dalip Singh was arrested and charged with the murder of his wife Inge. The trial was held six months later. It opened on November 1st before Mr. Justice Duke in the Hall of Justice, and the Crown, led by Mr. Malcolm Butt, contended that the motive for the crime was jealousy.

A private detective testified that Dr. Singh had asked him to tell his wife that she and a native assistant administrator for St.

Vincent had been shadowed and their actions had been witnessed. The witness told the court he had refused to be party to such a deception.

Slowly the prosecution's case was constructed out of bits and pieces of vital testimony. It was established that the Hindu doctor had met his wife at the Piarco airport when she returned from St. Vincent on the morning of April 6th. They drove to her bank, where she had withdrawn between six and seven hundred pounds. The Singhs' cook served them lunch and later dinner that same day, and the East Indian houseboy testified that in the evening he had heard the Singhs quarrelling bitterly in the garden and afterwards the sound of blows. The same witness said the doctor had driven away about a quarter past eight and had returned late, about two the next morning.

Various witnesses said Dr. Singh had told them his wife had left Port of Spain. One woman claimed he had been rude to her when she asked after Mrs. Singh. "Keep your nose out of our affairs," the Hindu told her, and then gratuitously informed her that his wife was having an affair with a man on St. Vincent.

Both Dr. Barrow and his wife Sylvia gave evidence for the Crown. Mrs. Barrow told of phone calls from Dr. Singh who wanted to speak to her husband urgently. They were made not long before the Hindu arrived at San Fernando, where the post mortem was being made.

The defence endeavoured to refute Dr. Barrow's testimony, claiming it was weighted by the witness's dislike of the prisoner because of the latter's treatment of Lucy Barrow. It equally sought to discount Lieutenant Clark's allegation that Dr. Singh had drafted the illiterate letter, but Reid's assistant demonstrated that the note had been written on paper taken from Dr. Singh's office, paper not sold in any of Trinidad's nearly thirty stationery shops.

The proceedings dragged on for nearly a month, and on the twenty-eighth day it closed, when the prisoner was found guilty and duly sentenced to death.

Seven months later, on June 28th 1955, Dalip Lutchmie Persad Singh was hanged in the yard of the Royal Jail. It was a day when, despite the rain, most of Trinidad seemed to be out in the streets, waiting to hear that retribution had overtaken the husband who had butchered his wife through insane jealousy.

12

THE CASE OF THE TOWPATH ASSASSIN

ON the last day of May 1953 two girls who were friends went for a cycle ride together. Barbara Songhurst was sixteen, Christine Reed eighteen. They had been talking in the morning about the forthcoming coronation of Queen Elizabeth II, which was to be on the following Tuesday.

Each girl expected to see the ceremony on TV. Neither did. They were by that time dead. Both had been wantonly murdered by a killer with a pathological passion for plunging steel into living flesh.

On the Saturday before they went on their tragic cycle ride the girls spent some time at Christine's home, which was at Hampton Hill. That was when they had discussed riding over to a camp at Log Farm. In the camp were some youths they knew. They rode over on their visit and the hours of that grim Sunday passed until it was almost Monday. Between eleven and eleven-thirty that night the girls were cycling along the towpath in the direction of Kingston Bridge. They rode on down the narrow track to meet violence.

About nine hours later, shortly before eight o'clock on the Monday morning, a man employed by the Port of London Authority saw something bulky in the Thames across from St. Catherine's Convent School. He approached as near as he could and made out a female body. It was floating just under the surface of the river.

He went and informed the police and a short while later a police launch moved up to where the body had been reported and the crew pulled the remains of Barbara Songhurst from the grey water.

Immediately the police began a search of the towpath paralleling the river. It did not take the searchers very long to find a place marked by splashes of recently spilled blood. There were similar splashes of blood on a green hedge, and grooved lines were traced where a body had been dragged to a bank after a knife attack of a most savage kind.

The police who had removed the body of Barbara Songhurst from the river had found four stab wounds in her back and they had observed wounds about the youthful head. It required a post mortem undertaken by Dr. A. K. Mant to provide more details about the dead girl's injuries.

Dr. Mant established that the girl had been murdered ten or twelve hours before her body was found floating in the river opposite the convent school. She had suffered a brutal clubbing on the head, but had actually died within a grim period of three to eight minutes from the stab wounds already noticed by the crew of the police launch.

She had also been raped.

A wound that offered something of a challenge to the pathologist conducting the post mortem was semicircular in shape. It was a blow that had been aimed at the victim's head, and one she had been unable to avoid, so it must have taken her by surprise, for it had smashed her left cheekbone. After the pathologist had considered this grim wound for a while he came to the conclusion that it could have been made with an axe-head.

He made some tests with blood samples taken from the place along the towpath where path and hedge were spattered with blood drops. Surprisingly he found the samples taken belonged to two separate groups, O and A.

Barbara Songhurst's blood belonged to the latter group.

A question was posed. Who was the person of blood group O who had bled where Barbara Songhurst was attacked by a determined assassin with a knife and an axe?

Was it the assassin?

The remaining question was, of course, where was Christine Reed, the younger girl's cycling companion, who had not reached home the previous night.

The next day Britain and the Commonwealth had their new queen crowned in Westminster Abbey. The newspapers were full of news about the event and the Abbey ceremony that was to be televised and recorded in colour film that would be dispatched around the world. Practically buried in the coronation news was the report on the finding of Barbara Songhurst's ravished and brutalised young body. It made a terribly grim few lines to offset the bright columns of vivid coronation reportage. But the brief reports on the latest murder in the London area ended with the announcement that the investigation was being conducted by Chief Inspector Herbert Hannam.

That Tuesday, June 2nd, 1953, was the fifth anniversary of the day when Bill Chapman and David Hislop went to Maidenhead where an old woman of ninety-four had been found under a mound of clothes in a black trunk.

It looked as though crime history was revealing a latent tendency to repeating itself. Also, a nice sense of timing. If Herbert Hannam was in no mind to appreciate such fine points that was understandable. He and his men, apart from workers in key industries, were some of the few in Britain that day who did a normal day's work. Only for them it was a normal day plus.

Hannam had a search of the river-banks and foreshore extended between Richmond and Kingston, and long before the bonfires were lit and the fireworks displays started his men, working with members of the Surrey Constabulary, were pursuing inquiries in a number of fête-minded Surrey villages and towns. They visited some Army camps and a camp occupied by American soldiers.

The G.I.s in their Bushey Park camp had a late visit. It was in the early hours of Wednesday that they were ordered to roll out of bed and get ready to answer questions by the police. Before their turn arrived visits had been paid to dance-halls and cinemas, restaurants and cafés, as well as the camp at Log Farm, where the two girl cyclists were known to have gone on a visit. The police on the case were beginning to accumulate a great deal of paper-work. The statements piled up, the questions and their answers had to be clipped together and given identity before being filed.

Hannam had not been on the case two days before he told his superiors at Scotland Yard, "This can take a long time."

The Yard detective was not being pessimistic. He was just not being falsely optimistic. That was the nature of the man. It was a built-in caution that was part of a profound thoroughness and belief in attention to detail, no matter how small it might be.

Hannam knew how little he had to go on in his hunt for a killer who liked slashing with cold steel, who was probably very mobile, for only someone able to get about easily would have been on the towpath so late on the Sunday night. Presumably he had been concealed in the bushes that were now waiting for summer rain to cleanse them of Barbara Songhurst's blood. He had been armed and alert, a man urged to violence and prepared to indulge it. He could have come from the direction of Teddington Lock.

The rain that washed the bushes of blood along the towpath began while the crowds were lining the streets and thoroughfares from Westminster Abbey to Buckingham Palace. It was continuing to fall when Hannam's men found a woman's bicycle in the reeds along one section of the muddy foreshore not far away. The cycle was removed and examined. Later it was identified as the cycle Christine Reed had ridden on the Sunday night.

The police still had to find what had become of the cycle's

owner. They also wanted to find Barbara Songhurst's cycle. A thorough search was made along the river in the neighbourhood of the place where the older girl's machine had been recovered. It proved to be time wasted. So was all the other time spent looking for the younger girl's cycle.

It was never found, and doubtless lies today concealed under the mud at the bottom of the Thames.

After all, the killer had been incredibly active and agile if he had disposed of two bodies after attacking both girls and had also got rid of their cycles. Of course, he could have dumped the older girl's cycle and ridden off on the other. This presupposed that he was on foot, which in turn would point to his not having a great range of operation.

Hence the round of intensive visits to town and villages and camps.

But for all the work being undertaken Herbert Hannam could not consider, a day or so after the coronation when the case was growing headlines in the papers, that he was making all the progress he might have expected. His warning to his Yard chiefs began to sound only too true.

He was specially interested to find a double-edged knife that was the killer's. Such a knife, according to Dr. Mant, had been used in stabbing the dead girl taken from the river. That was another disappointment Hannam was to retain throughout the investigation. The double-edged knife, like Barbara Songhurst's cycle, was never found. It could have followed the cycle into the mud at the bottom of the river.

Not that Hannam didn't try every way he knew of finding objects that would have proved valuable exhibits at a trial. He arranged for police launches to be specially equipped with magnetic drags. The launches went from bank to bank up and down the river in a close-knit pattern that covered all likely areas. He had patrols with trained dogs scour the fields and woods running inland for several miles from the Surrey bank of the Thames. On the day after the coronation teams were out in the damp undergrowth, scouring thickets and overgrown patches near the towpath with mine detectors. Hannam had told them, "Look for a bloodstained axe or a double-edged knife."

That Wednesday his men's backs ached, but they returned from their labours with empty hands.

Hannam set up a conference at Scotland Yard, where a group of detectives and specialists discussed all the implications of the post mortem report, in the hope that someone might come up with a suggestion that could prove useful at this stage of an investigation that was growing and spreading like a ripple on the surface of a lake.

When the conference closed an appeal was issued to the general public. Anyone who had been along the towpath after dark on the previous Sunday was requested to come forward and answer questions. The appeal was carried in the newspapers and broadcast by radio and TV stations. The hunt for Barbara Songhurst's killer was still headline news.

The mystery of what had become of her friend Christine Reed earned even larger headlines.

Herbert Hannam remained spotlighted in a bright glare of publicity. His secret hope was that the publicity turned up evidence. It was the one thing he was short of. He had hundreds of typed-out statements, but there was precious little in them that he could use.

While specialists continued at the Yard with the tests they were making on Christine Reed's cycle the man in charge of the overall investigation tried something else that was new and might conceivably be rewarding. He arranged for vocal tests to be made at various distances from the lodge of the keeper at Teddington Lock. The lock-keeper, John West, said he had heard no sound of a cry for help or a scream on the Sunday night, and it was his opinion that if someone had screamed or called out they must have been sufficiently far away for the sound to be lost in the other sound made by the river water pouring through the lock sluices. By his tests Hannam hoped to find at which radius such sounds were first lost in the gurgling noise of the sluice water.

The bloodstained section of the towpath was well outside the range at which cries could be distinguished from the lock-keeper's lodge. It was a negative point to prove, but Hannam was tirelessly refusing to avoid any possibility of coming by a clue.

The day after the vocal tests were made preparations were made to drain the Thames between Teddington Lock and Richmond. Before this work could be completed the report of the forensic scientists who had examined the cycle at the Yard was received by Hannam. It suggested that Christine Reed's cycle had collided with another, possibly Barbara Songhurst's.

To Hannam this held a suggestion supporting his own view that the killer had sprung at both girls as they were pedalling along in the dark. He had caused them to wobble and collide, and it was conceivable that Christine Reed had been the nearer and she had fallen off her cycle, which had its front wheel turned and continued rolling on towards the river until it went over the bank. In that event the killer would not have handled it.

Again a negative result helped only in a process of elimination, for the only fingerprints found on the cycle were those of the missing girl and her father. It sounds undramatic as a piece of routine police work, but to obtain this result a fresh way of taking fingerprints had to be evolved and put into practice. The cycle's frame had been baked for thirty-six hours, then the surfaces were specially treated to bring up latent impressions and these were photographed.

On June 5th the investigation underwent a fresh driving impetus. Hannam gave instructions for the men making house-to-house inquiries in Surrey to undertake the questioning of every householder on the large Ham estate on the Kingston side of Richmond.

As in the work of fingerprinting the recovered bicycle, a new procedure was evolved. For the first time in a Yard investigation each policeman and detective was to have an identical printed questionnaire. This would be filled in by the police officer, not by the person interviewed. In this way the police interviewer would be able to enlarge his field of questioning to obtain a precise answer to a question printed on the official form he had for completing.

There were seventeen questions, and between each was space in which the questioner could add comments or observations of his own. Both the person questioned and the police interrogator were to sign each form. It would then comprise a veritable statement in précis, as it were, with an official witness to what was said. Such filled-in forms could be valuable evidence in a subsequent trial if they contained vital information.

Among the most important questions on the form were the following:

"Were the two girls known to you?

When and where did you last see them alive?

Where were you between 10 p.m. and midnight on May 31st?

Give the names and addresses of anyone who can verify the above question.

Who did you see during those two hours and what were you doing?

What do you know of the girls and their associates?

Do you know of any persons visiting the neighbourhood, or resident there, who have gone away since Sunday?"

It could be possible from such a questionnaire to detect someone in a lie, for the lie would be on record.

It was an operation that Hannam thought might take as long as two working weeks to complete. By this time he was convinced that he was on a case where he could not afford to overlook any possibility of coming by information.

He was also personally holding to the conviction that the killer he sought was a person who must live a semi-nomadic life. He had arrived at this stage from studying a number of reports obtained by the Surrey police of women being scared by a male stranger who had leaped at them from behind cover in some lonely place. The man jumping at them had in each case brandished a weapon in a threatening manner. Some of the reports mentioned an axe.

Hannam was sure, without having the proof to support his belief, that this phantom who sprang out at women in different parts of the northern fringe of the county, bordering the river, was the man who had murdered Barbara Songhurst, and perhaps her missing friend.

From the accumulated reports of such scaring attacks the Yard man was also convinced that the male menace in the dark was both young and of athletic build. He had to be muscular, and the chances were he was physically very strong.

The week passed with the investigation still in top gear and Hannam waiting for the next development that would take it a good way forward.

On the Saturday it occurred, a grim and terrible development that brought on a rash of Fleet Street's largest headline type. Christine Reed's body was found about two miles from that bloodstained patch of towpath where she and her friend had been jumped by a killer who had slaughtered both of them.

The medical examination described a number of wounds made when the girl had tried to protect herself from the determined assassin. Besides these glancing wounds there were ten others, all deep, where a knife had been deliberately thrust into her body.

Three of those knife wounds had punctured her heart.

In addition, like her younger friend, she had been raped.

When the reporters came flocking Hannam told them in a hard voice, "There's been no similar kind of attack for seventy years."

He could have been alluding to the Jack the Ripper murders in Whitechapel back in the 1870's. As a considered comment, it revealed how grimly he felt about the case he was investigating—and the vicious killer he was determined to capture.

He turned the investigation to mental homes. A special list of men known to be sexually murderous was prepared, as well as another of violently dangerous men. Every man on the latter was visited by a plain-clothes officer and invited to make a statement. Every man on the former was checked at the mental home or institution where he was detained. It was estimated that at this time Hannam was directing the largest force of detectives ever deployed on one murder case in Britain. He had half a dozen men working full time on indexing crimes with similar features. The door-to-door officers with their questionnaires had had their numbers trebled. The statements by this time were arriving in thousands, rather than mere hundreds. The paper-work was becoming mountainous.

Hannam had become convinced of another thing. The man he sought lived locally. Only a local could have got himself home and cleaned up after the bloody slaughter of the girls on the tow-path. A score of daggers and knives were found. None was the one Hannam was hoping to find.

Fresh inquiries were started at Surrey factories and calls were made up and down the river on houseboat dwellers. On June 10th the draining of the Thames began with the help of the river's conservancy board. The operation started at five a.m. and by nine-thirty the river was at its lowest level. Scores of police in gumboots explored the exposed reaches. A special water-glass, a long cylinder nine inches in diameter with a ground-glass lens in its base, was employed as a sort of submarine telescope. The great river search failed to find the distinctive double-edged knife or Barbara Songhurst's cycle.

New appeals appeared on cinema screens in Surrey on the 13th. After that the newspapers began to lose interest. Hannam became drained of immediate news value. The days stretched into weeks, while the investigation continued. The weeks became months. Two months and a week passed after those appeals were made on cinema screens within a ten-mile radius of where the crime had been committed. Then the case was back in the headlines. Hannam was news again.

So was a certain Alfred Charles Whiteway. On Thursday,

August 10th, he was arrested and charged at Richmond magistrates' court with the murders of Barbara Songhurst and Christine Rose Reed. The hearing lasted barely four minutes and then the prisoner was driven to Brixton Prison.

The formal hearing in the magistrates' court opened nearly a month later on September 15th. The Crown's counsel presented evidence that the back of an axe had been found by Dr. Mant to fit two skull fractures sustained by one victim. He told the court:

"On June 17th two police officers saw Whiteway on Oxshott Common and invited him to go to Kingston police station. When he got there he was imediately allowed to go. When he travelled down in the police car he sat in the back, alone. The two police officers sat in the front. The following day another police officer was preparing to take the car out when he found an axe under the driver's seat. He took the axe and placed it in his locker, and some little while later took it home with him. On one occasion he used it to chop wood, so the axe is somewhat blunt, for when he did chop wood it was on a hard surface. That axe was not, in fact, handed to Detective Superintendent Hannam, who was in charge of the case, until July 15th."

Before that day when Mr. J. F. Claxton told this amazing story Hannam had been promoted to superintendent. But he was a man who could have had better luck. For two months he had been trying to find a murderer and a weapon. The latter was in a police officer's home, being used to chop firewood.

There is a fitting corollary to this almost unprecedented set of circumstances in a murder hunt. At the trial of Whiteway at the Central Criminal Court a month later the police driver who removed the axe from the car without notifying anyone fainted when his name was called to give evidence.

But for the disappearance of the murder weapon Hannam would have made his arrest weeks earlier. He had noted that a week before the murders, on May 24th, a girl of fifteen had been attacked on Oxshott Common. She had afterwards given the police a reasonably clear description of the athletic young man who had jumped on her. On June 12th a woman was similarly sprung upon in Windsor Great Park. She had pushed her handbag into the face of a dark-haired, clean-shaven man wearing dungarees and large brown gloves. While he was fumbling with the handbag's catch she ran away. There were other and similar attacks, going back into the previous year. Hannam became more and more certain that the same athletic young man was the culprit in each case.

The publicity given the case led indirectly to the arrest, for Hannam had kept giving out information on each development to the Press. Because a couple of workmen had read about the young man in dungarees and brown gloves they recognised the description when they saw a young man loitering on Oxshott Common. They reported the young man to the police and a radio car was summoned. The man was picked up and put in the police car. He had slipped an axe under a leather jacket. On the way to be questioned, as was discovered much later, he had pushed the axe down on the floor of the car.

Whiteway should have been in custody that night. Instead, he was allowed to leave a police station—but without his axe. Inspector Leonard Bramhall had taken his name at Kingston. Whiteway had said he was married and a father, but because he and his young wife of eighteen could not find accommodation she was living with her family and he with his.

He answered the inspector's questions, and there was no obvious reason for detaining him. It was not until the description of the man who had attacked the woman in Windsor Great Park was circulated that the penny dropped at Kingston. There was suddenly a hurry to question Whiteway again.

Plain-clothes men called at his home in Sydney Road, Teddington, and were told he was out. He was out each time they called. A message was left for him to keep an appointment made for him. He failed to turn up. He managed to evade the police until June 28th, when he was arrested. The towpath murders were not referred to. It was Hannam who opened up that subject with the prisoner. Whiteway denied knowing anything about the crime. He appeared in court and was committed for trial charged with the assault on Oxshott Common. Meanwhile the all-important axe was in a woodshed in a police driver's garden.

It would have changed everything for Hannam, but he didn't know it had been found.

By this time two hundred C.I.D. men had been actively engaged on the case. Specialists had been flown to Washington by the F.B.I. to help trace repatriated American G.I.s who had been stationed at the Bushey Park camp. All over the country an effort was being made to trace a woman's Phillips bicycle No. K 29421, size twenty-one inch, with a maroon frame and cream mudguards with gilt lines, three-quarter drop handlebars, three-speed gear, half chain guard and chromium caliper-type brakes. That cycle had been the pride of sixteen-year-old Barbara Songhurst.

Hannam dug out the salient facts in Whiteway's background simply because he wanted everything he could get about a man who fitted the case, but against whom he could, as yet, prove no connection with the towpath murders.

He discovered that Whiteway was one of a family of nine children. Their father had died in 1945. Whiteway had gone to a primary school in Teddington, where he was remembered for his love of knives. During the war he had been evacuated to South Wales. He had been in and out of one job after another at frequent intervals since leaving school, but had learned no trade and was unskilled. He had even been rejected for National Service on account of defective vision and virulent acne. The maximum range of his normal vision was about eighty yards. He had sought jobs near his home and had once taken a job in Oxshott. He had met his unlucky wife while walking by the river and they were married in February 1952. She was seventeen. In the following May her first child was born, and the family had to leave their Kingston flat, where they had been known as Ross. Without a home, the young family had split up, leaving Whiteway free to ride his cycle where he liked and carry with him in his saddle bag an axe and a double-edged knife.

Hannam even located a Greenford schoolmaster who had seen a young man he had identified as Whiteway throwing knives and an axe at a tree near Richmond on a Sunday morning. He had been asked to try his own skill by the knife-thrower. Humouring the young man, the schoolmaster had thrown a curved small knife and missed the target so completely the knife had gone into a pit partly filled with water. Whiteway had gone after it, but had not found it.

On instructions from Hannam, Inspector Vivian of Richmond found that missing knife after the pit was drained. A mine detector located the weapon. It proved to be a Gurkha kukri.

Hannam had another point cleared up. That second blood sample in Group O. Both Whiteway and Christine Reed had blood in that group.

Then the axe turned up.

Just how Hannam took its late arrival is not known, which is possibly just as well. But he lost no time in taking it to Brixton Prison, where Whiteway was being held on remand while the tireless search went on.

Whiteway looked at it with shock etched into his face. He had suddenly grown much older than his twenty-two years. Hannam, however, had come prepared to build up the pressure. He not only had the axe, but he told the shocked young man that the Yard's forensic science experts had found blood traces on one of his shoes. At that Whiteway underwent emotional collapse. He made a statement that was tantamount to a confession.

Then reaction set in. He was told frankly that Barbara Songhurst's cycle had not been found, nor had the double-edged knife. Hannam was hoping Whiteway would clear up what had become of them. Instead, the prisoner tried to retract his statement. He claimed he had been tricked. He also said he had an alibi. He had been with his wife at the time of the towpath murders.

But he couldn't make it sound even halfway convincing.

The Old Bailey trial opened on October 26th before Mr. Justice Hilbery. It became a legal wrangle with rough undertones. Mr. Peter Rawlinson, a former Irish Guards officer, led for the defence, which incorporated an attack on Whiteway's statement, which the judge had admitted as evidence.

"I say with great seriousness," the defence counsel stated, "that there have been most serious allegations made by me against a superintendent of police and a detective sergeant, because if Whiteway never made that statement the only explanation is that it was fabricated by somebody, and it is suggested his signature got on it by means of a trick. That defence is only put before you on the unequivocal evidence of Whiteway, who said he never made that statement."

Criminal history, it seems, repeats itself inside court as well as out. Five years before a defence counsel had attacked Chapman and Cherrill in the trial of George Russell. Now it was Hannam's turn to hear police officers challenged and their integrity questioned. As in the case of the trial of George Russell, so in Whiteway's, the judge felt constrained to deal with the attitude of the defence towards the police. When Mr. Justice Hilbery summed up for the jury, he referred to the statement, saying, "Was it the sudden outburst of a man who was deeply conscious of his guilt and who had kept that consciousness locked in his own breast until there came a moment when he must purge his bosom of the stuff that poisons the heart?"

As he paused the judge held up the actual confesssion offered in evidence.

"Look at the statement," he went on. "Do you think that an experienced novelist, a writer of fiction, could have done much better than that? It is said to have been done by a police officer."

He waved the statement.

"Well!" he exclaimed and dropped it on the bench in front of him.

He returned to the statement in his closing remarks.

"If he did say it," said the judge, "it is a confession and he is guilty. There is no escaping from that. If he did not say it you are faced with one of the most wicked pieces of evidence I should think has ever been made in this country, and certainly one of the most wicked pieces that has ever been before me."

The jury retired to consider their verdict after the lunch adjournment. When they left their seats in court it was not only Whiteway who was on trial, but also, as Mr. Christmas Humphreys who led for the prosecution had pointed out to them in his last address, the good name and honour of a police officer with a great and distinguished career.

The jury, which comprised ten men and two women, were out thirty-five minutes considering their verdict. After that interval they returned to ask the learned judge for advice.

They wanted to be quite clear about whether the axe had been on the table in the room in Brixton Prison where Superintendent Hannam interviewed Whiteway on July 30th. The judge consulted his notes on the testimony given and informed them that the evidence had been that Hannam had taken the axe from his briefcase and then put it back. In short, Whiteway had seen his own property and had recognised it.

The jury retired again. They were absent forty-seven minutes before they returned and the foreman announced that they had found the prisoner guilty.

Whiteway's appeal against the verdict was dismissed by the Lord Chief Justice, Lord Goddard, who spoke of the axe and the statement Whiteway had made after seeing it in Hannam's possession.

"I am going to read the whole of this document," said Lord Goddard, "to know what filthy expressions are in it."

He proceeded to read the statement through with obvious distaste, and then asked rhetorically, "Could ever a play of the bloody Lady Macbeth have been brought out in real life more than in this case?"

The Old Bailey verdict and the dismissal of Whiteway's appeal completely vindicated Herbert Hannam from the slur passed on his conduct in the presentation of Whiteway's defence.

He had a right to expect that full vindication.

He had worked untiringly and undauntedly to remove a menace to any woman alone at night in North Surrey. The tow-path murderer was hanged at Wandsworth on November 22nd, just over three weeks after a jury had found him guilty of a particularly bestial crime. One of the weapons he used, a blunt axe with an almost incredible story of misadventure, eventually arrived in Scotland Yard's famous Black Museum.